Two
for Joy

D1149809

James Melville-Ross is, he c͟ an unremarkable individual in every respect, save for th ͟ ͟ ͟ ͟ sing of being the father of two extraordinary children. Having severely disabled twins makes him interesting for the first time in his life . . .

Since the twins' diagnosis, James has become a disability bore. He has given speeches at Downing Street and at the Houses of Parliament, written blogs and articles. The more he told the twins' story, the more he began to realise what a powerful tool their tale is for righting misconceptions and ignorance about disability.

Storytelling runs in James's veins – his grandfather was a novelist, and he is a descendant of Herman Melville, the author of *Moby Dick*. He is realistic about the long shadow cast by his ancestors, but everyone loves a trier . . .

He and his wife, Georgie, live with their family in Buckinghamshire.

Two for Joy

The true story of one family's
journey to happiness with severely
disabled twins

James Melville-Ross

JOHN BLAKE

Published by John Blake Publishing Limited,
3 Bramber Court, 2 Bramber Road,
London W14 9PB, England

www.johnblakebooks.com

www.facebook.com/johnblakebooks [f]
twitter.com/jblakebooks [t]

First published in paperback in 2016

ISBN: 978-1-78606-010-5

All rights reserved. No part of this publication may be reproduced, stored in a
retrieval system, or transmitted in any form or by any means, without the prior
permission in writing of the publisher, nor be otherwise circulated in any form
of binding or cover other than that in which it is published and without a similar
condition including this condition being imposed on the subsequent purchaser.

British Library Cataloguing-in-Publication Data:
A catalogue record for this book is available from the British Library.

Design by www.envydesign.co.uk

Printed in Great Britain by CPI Group (UK) Ltd

1 3 5 7 9 10 8 6 4 2

© Text copyright James Melville-Ross 2016

The right of Jam ... the author of this work has been
asserted by him ... with the Copyright, Designs and Patents ... 1988.

Papers used by John Blake Publishing are natural, recyclable products made from
wood grown in ... manufacturing processes conform to the
environmental ... of the country of origin.

Every attempt ... has been made to contact ... copyright holders, but some
were unobtaina ... If any have been inadvertently overlooked ... contact us.

LANCASHIRE COUNTY
LIBRARY

3011813364324 1

Askews & Holts	15-Jun-2016
306.874092 MEL	£7.99
CLE	

For Georgie
If they asked me, I could write a book
About the way you walk and whisper and look.
'I COULD WRITE A BOOK', LORENZ HART, 1940

Contents

Prologue

Tonight's the night.

The planets are aligned, Jupiter is in ascent; horseshoes, four-leafed clover and rabbit's feet have been acquired. Surely there won't be a better time to do it than right now.

Georgie and I have been trying for a baby for three years. Our first course of IVF was a disaster, an abject and humiliating failure, but we've decided to go again. Tonight is the night we're going to see whether the second IVF treatment has worked.

While Georgie prepares the pregnancy test at home I take our dog to the park. Partly it's because the dog needs some air, partly because I need some too.

After years of failing to conceive I have become very superstitious, tiptoeing over the cracks in the pavement as we make our way along the suburban street to our local park. As I enter the park, just for good measure, I look heavenwards and send up a prayer to a God I don't yet fully believe in.

A magpie appears, hopping along the weed-bound, paved path.

'Shit,' I mutter to myself. 'Bad sign – *one for sorrow.*'

Superstitious thoughts again as the rhyme runs through my head:

'One for sorrow, two for joy, three for a girl, four for a boy.'

But wait, here's another magpie – *two for joy*!

Then a third and a fourth – *three for a girl, four for a boy*!

I stand, momentarily transfixed, and wonder what this means.

PART 1

LIFE
SUPPORT

1. Wednesday, 27 August

The doors to the delivery suite bang open as Georgie's bed is rolled in.

The room is huge. There must be fifteen people in here, a small army of obstetricians, anaesthetists, neonatal doctors, nurses and midwives, and they are in a whirlwind of preparation, activity and order. My heart jumps to see so many people and I'm momentarily panicked by the sheer scale of the process that has been put in place for the arrival of our twins. But everywhere I turn I see calm, relaxed faces – faces which say this is normal for us – all in a day's work.

Georgie's frail frame is tilted forward as the epidural is administered and she shudders as the long needle slides into her spinal column. I perch anxiously alongside her on the bed as the anaesthetic starts to take effect.

The tall, young anaesthetist's face wears the same pained expression that we have seen on the faces of all of the doctors sent to talk to us over the previous five days of labour. I notice his bad teeth as he says, 'The lives of such premature babies are rarely uncomplicated . . . You do realise that you are both in for a very long and difficult journey, don't you?'

We nod the nods of people who want to look like they know what everyone's on about – nods we have perfected in the last few days. We frown in a way which is intended to indicate that we absolutely understand the seriousness of the task ahead of us.

We will laugh about this later. Laugh at our naivety and our stupidity for trying to look like we had the remotest idea what was about to happen to us.

*

The anaesthetic has taken effect, Georgie is ready and suddenly we are in business. Within seconds the sun roof is being peeled back, bringing light and life to our twins.

The surgeon is shrouded behind the curtain that crosses Georgie's chest, but the direction of his voice changes as he leans in to grasp the first of our babies and says, 'Feels a bit like someone rummaging around in your handbag . . . you know it's happening but it doesn't hurt.'

My face is close to Georgie's as she winces in discomfort, more at the thought of what's going on, rather than pain. I feel strangely elated about the thought of finally meeting our children and I smile.

I whisper, 'I love you,' and she weakly returns my smile. I squeeze her hand, pleased that this chapter is almost over and the trauma of her five days of labour can end.

I'm eager to catch a glimpse of our newborns for the first

time and I raise my head above the line of the sheet. The calm, peaceful sanctuary of our private moment together vanishes as I contemplate the battle scene in front of me.

I breathe in sharply.

Georgie's stomach, untimely ripped from side to side, is now a gaping hole. The yellow belly fat of her half-pregnancy glistens brightly in sharp contrast to the dark red blood that runs from her wound. And there, in the midst of it all, two blue-gloved hands tear my wriggling son from the safe harbour of the womb.

'A boy!' the doctor shouts, triumphantly.

My boy, I think.

He is momentarily held aloft and time stands still for a split second.

He is tiny and he squeaks like a mouse as he takes his first breath. I can't believe he's human. He looks like a tiny tangle of intestines. Did the doctor yank the wrong bit out?

One side of the room bursts into a flurry of activity. The baby is wrapped in swaddling and rushed over to a small trolley where a team of nurses descends on him, desperate to use these few, decisive moments to save his life.

My mouth hangs open as I turn back to Georgie. Clearly this is not the expression she was looking for from me.

'And a girl!' shouts the surgeon and she too is whisked off to another corner to be resuscitated.

'A boy and a girl!' I say to Georgie, who smiles back at me. Finally her part of the ordeal is over.

A nurse rushes across. 'Would you like to hold your baby girl?' she says to Georgie.

'Yes, please,' comes the eager reply. After days of battling to keep these babies on board, finally the moment has arrived when she gets her reward of meeting them. A nurse brings our baby daughter over and places her against Georgie's neck.

Georgie's face is a look of sheer panic.

'Oh my God, she's tiny!' she says, her eyes flaring with fright and her hands shaking as she cradles the baby in her neck. Our daughter is so tiny, it looks as though Georgie is cradling a telephone handset beneath her chin, rather than holding a newborn. She looks up to me, her face begging for the reassurance I'm just not qualified to give.

'They're going to be fine,' I say, stroking Georgie's hair, my smile betrayed by the panic she must surely see in my eyes.

And before we know it, the nurse has whisked our daughter away and the battle for our twins' lives begins.

2. April

It was a hot spring day, just three months earlier, when the obstetrician confirmed the joyous news that the blue cross on the pregnancy kit had suggested to us that night with the magpies.

I remember the sun warming my smiling face as Georgie and I hugged on the pavement after the appointment. It's an embrace we have perfected over the years – Georgie, nearly a foot shorter than me, her face buried in my chest, my long arms wrapped almost twice around her slim frame. And for the first time in almost three years it was a hug of celebration, rather than consolation.

It was the first time since Georgie and I set out on our journey to start a family that our expectations were exceeded, rather than undershot. We had years of trying and eventually succumbed to the need for IVF when they told us that we were 'completely incompatible as partners'. It seemed ironic to me that we were so entirely compatible in every sense, but not in this – the most critical area, baby making.

And even then, once we made that decision, each month our hopes were raised as Georgie passed the day her period normally arrived, only to be dashed when it started again. The plunge back to square one, the tears and reassurances as the cycle of rebuilding began: until next month, when hope would buoy us up again.

But now, with a bit of a shove and a fair following wind, we were going to become the proud parents of not one, but two children. As we hugged on the pavement, I squeezed Georgie tight and for the first time I got the new and peculiar sensation that two lives were now growing between us.

Even the surrounding buildings seemed to nod their knowing support for the news we had just been given – delivered by our obstetric doctor in an inappropriately deadpan manner.

'Yes, definitely two heartbeats,' she had said as if dispensing a prescription.

In that darkened room, lit only by the lamp aimed between Georgie's legs, we heard the news we had waited years to hear and in an instant the clouds lifted and we were left wondering what all the fuss had been about.

For me the pain had been limited to mind games: three years of trying to conceive and the slowly increasing panic that this was never going to happen for us. Reassuring Georgie every month that everything would be OK in the end, whilst never having any kind of certainty myself.

All that worry was gone in a flash.

The almost indecipherable shapes on the screen were explained to us, 'You see the head, the limb buds [yuk!] and the heartbeat?' The heartbeat, a tiny constellation of dots flickering on and off – as difficult for us to comprehend as some distant galaxy viewed through a telescope. Our eyes strained to see and our minds strained to believe what we were witnessing.

In this dim-lit lab, perched on top of Georgie's discarded trousers and pants, I grasped her hand and we gawped at each other like game-show winners who can't believe their luck.

'Hey, remember I told you about the magpies?' I said. 'One for sorrow, two for joy, three for a girl, four for a boy? Maybe we're having one of each – a boy and a girl?'

'Wonder what the first one means.' Georgie asked.

'I guess the sorrow is the pain we've gone through to get here,' I replied.

That must be right. Nothing can possibly go wrong now. We've done it. We've finally bloody done it!

And the postscript of an email from my brother says everything about how we and our family feel about this moment . . .

'PS TWINS!!!'

3. July

In the ten years that I've known Georgie, I've never known her have anything other than a beautifully smooth, flat stomach. But my heart swells with pride to see her now, a small bump telling of the long-longed-for presence of our twins.

We met in the first week of university and while all our friends were jumping from bed to bed, we quietly and slowly fell in love, talking endlessly over subsidised breakfast bacon sandwiches and cheap pancake dinners about our friends, our passions and our dreams. She took me on, despite my Mohican, my hideous fashion sense and horizontal approach to life. And I fell in love with her, even as she refused immediate access to the one thing that all nineteen-year-old boys are interested in. So I spent my early days doing everything in my power to make her sure about me. Later, drunk at a house party, I spilt red wine on her white shirt and she slapped me. I thought, I might have to marry this girl.

Within months, we had introduced one another to each other's families. Georgie is the third of four daughters, the ballsiest of five strong women in a loud and loving family. At the head of the family is Serena, a fun-loving, huge-hearted Australian who welcomed me into the family with open arms and immediately put me at ease, calling me 'darling' in her Dame Edna brogue. Georgie's father, Bobs, the quintessential English gent, quickly became something of a hero to all the boyfriends (and eventual husbands) of his daughters . . . After all, we only had one each to contend with! He had developed a streak of mischief which I soon realised was the ideal coping mechanism for survival in this female-dominated household.

I'm the middle of three kids. My older brother, Rupert, and I had a fiercely competitive upbringing. I was the younger, cockier brother and believed I was as good as him until I was fifteen, when he put any delusions of parity to bed by landing a haymaker on my chin and dropping me on my backside after an argument. We instantly became best friends.

Our younger sister, Emma, watched this peacocking with amused detachment and, for the most part, let us get on with it. Three years younger than me, she taught us to be loving and caring and grew up with a hardy constitution as a result of having to compete with her brothers for food and attention.

Mum is the driving influence for us and the force behind the safe cocoon of a strong and loving family unit. A more loving mother one could not hope to have, always teaching, always pressing and always instilling in us an attitude that you should throw yourself into everything. Who knows where it might lead?

Dad is an equally critical influence – a hugely successful

businessman, he was made Chief Executive of Nationwide Building Society aged just thirty-nine. We turn to him in times of drama and he always seems to have the answers. Despite his success, Dad is never more than two steps away from doing something ludicrous. I like to kid myself that my gorilla impression is on a par with his, but, to be honest, the facial contortions he manages to pull put his in a different class.

After university, Georgie and I had stayed together; trundling along a course that we both secretly knew would end in marriage. We were happy for it to be so. Georgie started her career in marketing and I set off into the financial PR industry and despite our different characteristics, we became ever closer friends and companions until the day finally dawned when I realised that I didn't ever want to spend another moment apart from her.

I proposed in a field near my parents' house, overlooking the Stour valley in Suffolk. I hit a cowpat as I went down on one knee and she laughed and then cried before eventually saying yes.

It rained on the day we got married. My great-aunt collapsed in the church and we had to call an ambulance. My speech was unfunny and ordinary. So many imperfections on what I now only remember as such a perfect day.

The single wonder of the day was the fact of marrying Georgie. The moment that she came into the church I was completely surprised to see her in a wedding dress. I couldn't take my eyes off her as she walked down the aisle and suddenly my nerves settled; this morning's reappearing breakfast now a distant memory. Now she's with me, it's all going to be OK.

*

Here we are, ten years after meeting, married for four, and about to become parents at last. We decided to take a last holiday together and excitedly booked a week's escape to Sardinia.

It's a hazy, sunny day on the beach and I'm lying back on my sun lounger, my head fogged by the combination of the warm conditions, a large lunch and a glass of wine.

Georgie approaches through my misted vision and sits beside me on the lounger.

'I hope they have your eyes.' She smiles and plants a kiss.

'Let's hope it's their mother they take after!' I reply, taking in Georgie's bewitching beauty. Angular cheekbones above dimpled cheeks that seem to be permanently smiling. And eyes that sparkle like the sun shimmering on the Sardinian sea.

'Boy and a girl, two boys or two girls?' I ask, putting a possessive arm around her midriff, around my family.

'I don't care, as long as they're healthy,' she replies and she's right. We have waited so long to be granted permission to become parents, it doesn't seem right to make any further requests.

'Me neither,' I confess. 'I still can't believe it. Twins!'

'I know, incredible.' She smiles and looks away into the distant sea, imagining.

'I've just been reading the twin book,' she says, the thought suddenly occurring to her. 'It says that by the time I'm full term, it will feel like the equivalent of drinking nineteen pints without going to the loo.'

We burst out laughing. 'That sounds pretty uncomfortable!' I say. 'I reckon I've held on to four pints before, but nineteen! Ouch!'

*

And now, finally, comes the relief of being able to talk about the trials of the IVF process with our friends. It has been hard for us to fix our faces with smiles of approval at our friends' baby news. But our faux delight has meant that they have all been oblivious to our attempts to conceive – easily dissuaded from pursuing questions about our plans for a family by our cheery reassurances that 'There'll be plenty of time for that – we're just enjoying being a couple.'

Yeh, whatever.

One Saturday evening, I open the front door to the whirlwind of giddy laughter and nonsense that is my collection of good friends from university – Steve, Eddie, Neil and Malcolm.

We settle around the table in our tiny London back garden as I begin the process of cooking their dinner on the barbecue.

Eventually, inevitably, talk turns to the pregnancy.

Intrigued by the concept of test-tube babies, Malcolm asks, 'So, how does it all work then, Jimmers?'

'Well, it's not a straightforward undertaking,' I explain. 'People tend to focus on the cost of the thing. Admittedly, that's a factor, but the physical side is far more of an undertaking.'

'What do you mean?' asks Neil, rocking back in his chair.

'Well, first of all Georgie had the lithotripsy – an operation to clear out the pipes and make sure everything's operating inside. Pretty nasty, very painful.'

'Oooh, sounds uncomfortable.' He grimaces, glancing at Georgie.

'Then, once the process started, Georgie had to inject her leg every day to give the eggs the best chance of developing fully. Not nice, every day jabbing the syringe into her thigh. She was stoic about it.'

I smile at Georgie, hoping that she doesn't mind me sharing these very personal details. She returns my smile in recognition of the silent request and I continue.

'Then there's the process where the sperm gets shot up as far as possible inside. You should see the kit they use! You have to have a full bladder for the operation – something to do with ensuring the shape of the womb is ideally positioned to receive the sperm. Georgie nearly passed out on the tube on the way there because she'd drunk so much water and over-hydrated.'

'Some old boy had to help me up the escalator.' Georgie laughs. 'Pretty embarrassing being helped off the tube by someone twice your age.'

We all laugh, then I continue, 'But the really nasty bit, several weeks later, was the farming procedure where they take the fertilised eggs out. This involves a scraping process to make sure they get as many as possible. After the operation, Georgie threw up out of the car window on the way home, she was in such pain.'

'Shit,' says Steve. 'I had no idea. Poor you, Georgie, it sounds like a nightmare.'

Her shrug and wry smile suggest a nonchalance that betrays the reality of what she has been through.

Eddie, ever the sensitive one, then asks, 'And what about you, Jimmers? What did you have to do?'

'Me?' I reply. 'Oh. I had to wank into a cup.'

4. August

The first indication that something is wrong with the pregnancy comes with a Friday lunchtime phone call from Georgie. She is five and a half months' pregnant, just twenty-four weeks in.

She tells me through faltering breaths that she has started bleeding.

'I've spoken to the hospital and they want me to go in.'

'Oh, shit,' I say. 'What's happening?'

'I don't know, J,' she replies, her voice starting to waver with panic. 'Please hurry!'

'Yes, of course. Absolutely. See you there. Shit.'

My head whirls with the possibilities as I jump into a taxi. What can this mean? Bleeding during pregnancy – doesn't sound good, but what do I know?

The glass half full – perhaps it's nothing. Maybe this happens during pregnancy. There's been so much activity going on with

Georgie's tummy and pipes, it stands to reason that there may have been some trauma. I'm sure it's nothing.

The glass half empty – but doesn't bleeding during pregnancy trigger labour? Isn't that supposed to come at the end of the process? We are little more than halfway through the pregnancy. Surely it can't be happening already?

I arrive at the hospital and I race from the taxi, up the lift on the sixth floor of St Thomas' Hospital, next to Westminster Bridge in London, and into a side room in the pre-natal department. Georgie is flat on the hospital bed and a nurse and obstetrician stand alongside, preparing to scan her tummy to check for signs of life.

Georgie shivers as the cold gel is smoothed across her tummy – still barely swollen despite the two lives inside her. The shiver is not because of the gel.

I walk across and squeeze her hand with a smile that is intended to reassure her.

'What does this mean?' I ask the doctor. A simple question, posed to a complete stranger, the answer to which will have such a profound impact on our happiness.

No answer. The doctor continues his fiddling with the equipment.

The scanning equipment crackles into life. Gradually the reassuring thump of a heartbeat can be heard.

'Is that both or just one?' I ask, trying, failing to hide the panic in my throat.

Finally he speaks: 'They're both fine.'

Relief. I squeeze Georgie's hand.

'So can you tell us what's going on here?'

'Well it looks like the placenta has torn and that's what's

causing the bleeding. Too much bleeding and eventually the body responds by going into labour, so it's important that you rest up now and allow it time to heal. Just as a precaution, I'm going to recommend that you stay here at the hospital for now. The next few days will be critical in determining whether the wound heals or labour starts.'

'Oh. Sorry. We're only at twenty-four weeks. Surely we're at risk of a miscarriage at this stage?' I say.

'We're not at that stage yet,' he says. 'Like I said, it's important that you get rest.'

*

The contractions kick in less than twenty-four hours later. Georgie's body begins to convulse with the spasms.

The same obstetrician arrives shortly, wheeling a scanner. He takes his time and we hear the crackle of heartbeats through the ultrasound and pray that our untrained ears are hearing two hearts.

Eventually he says, 'The twins are fine, but as you will have guessed, things have not improved in the way that we had hoped they would. We must prepare for something happening soon.'

'But we've still got four months to go . . . ?' Georgie says, disbelieving.

'We're most likely looking at a relatively near term arrival, so we need to be ready for that now.'

He sees our blank, uncomprehending faces and continues.

'There's every chance the twins will arrive in the coming days. I'm sorry. This is going to be hard for all of you.'

All of us. Yes, I remind myself that there are more than two people in this family to think about now.

He continues, 'We have to take every pang, every bleed seriously at this stage, but what we're secretly hoping for is that the twins stay on board for as long as possible. Every day counts for children born this early.'

'What chance do they have of surviving at just twenty-four weeks?' I ask.

'We'll have someone come and talk to you about that at the right time.'

It feels like the right time might be really rather soon, but we nod and assume that the experts know what they are doing.

By Sunday night, Georgie is slipping in and out of consciousness and preparations are made for the twins' arrival. More jabs – this time steroids to open the babies' lungs and drugs to calm the contractions to try to prevent the babies' arrival.

At times the drugs are causing Georgie's heart to race to such an extreme that I am becoming very concerned about her ability to cope with the demands being put on her body.

*

Our families have been itching to try to help and so now Georgie's younger sister, Alice, has joined us to support Georgie. Alice and I feel as useless as each other as we watch this tsunami approaching, knowing that there's so little we can do about it. We stand in the corridor together while Georgie sleeps and ask ourselves questions that we can't possibly answer yet.

What *is* now clear is that if things continue to deteriorate, our as-yet unnamed, unknown twins will be arriving very soon. Even though the babies continue to kick and their heartbeats plod on, the chances of them surviving for much longer in utero are disappearing fast.

On the other hand, Georgie has now spent several days in labour. I feel deep concern for her physical wellbeing, but almost more worrying is her refusal to allow herself to show too much emotion during this marathon. Tears stream down her face with the pain, but from the neck down she is trying to keep as calm as possible so as not to further upset the babies. She is battling to suppress her emotions and to provide as calm an environment as possible for them. It seems she has gone onto autopilot, refusing to let these events get on top of her and determined to do everything in her power to save her babies. I've never seen a more remarkable demonstration of bravery.

Outside, the small sphere of our family and friends waits on tenterhooks. My parents have moved down from Suffolk to their London flat nearby and pace the floors, anxiously waiting for news. Georgie's parents are on holiday and desperate to return to be with us, but Georgie dissuades them.

'It's all going to be fine,' I hear her reassuring her mother on the phone. 'I'm absolutely convinced of it.'

And she is as well. She seems to be determined that all this will be over in a few days and that we will return home to continue the pregnancy where we left off. I have a creeping sense that she is in denial.

The texts of support from friends are lovely but go unanswered. After all, what can I say? Outside, the world continues its bustle, oblivious to the dramas unfolding inside our bubble.

All the time, the same, unanswered, question keeps returning to my mind – how early can a baby be born and still survive?

Each scan reveals their little heartbeats continuing to thump faintly through the sonar, each new doctor tells us that they are hanging in there, but no one seems to want to be specific about what our babies' chances of survival will be.

On Tuesday night my question is answered.

The door of our hospital cubicle opens to a doctor dressed in ordinary clothes, but with the official badge of the hospital on a lanyard around her neck. From her manner it is clear that she is here to talk business and Alice, reading the situation, makes her excuses and leaves our room. The doctor introduces herself as Silky and explains that she is one of the registrars from the neonatal unit. She tells us that she has come to explain what will happen when the twins arrive.

'The main areas of concern will be the three vital organs – the brain, the heart and the lungs,' she begins in a staccato voice. 'The twins' lungs will definitely be damaged because they are not yet formed at twenty-four weeks' gestation. But lungs we can deal with. We are most worried about damage to the heart or brain during the first seventy-two hours.'

I can't take my eyes off the single sheet of paper she put on Georgie's bed when she first came in. I can see a bar chart outlining the survival rates for premature babies. *What does it say? What chance do they have?*

Eventually she turns to the chart. She lifts it off the bed and now I see what she has been working up to. I can't help but notice the alarming drop-off in survival percentages prior to twenty-six weeks.

'Babies born at twenty-four weeks have a twenty per cent chance of survival. Of those that survive, half suffer brain damage of some type,' she delivers blankly. She's been through this countless times before but for us it's the first time. I imagine her team deciding who does this job. Do they draw straws? What a horrible lottery. Silky's warmth will become very evident to us in the coming weeks, but for now we are struck by how detached she appears.

Do I really want to ask this question? Before I can stop myself, it's out. 'So what you're saying is that we have a five per cent chance of ending up with two healthy babies?'

She's well-rehearsed on this one. 'The statistics are to help provide you with some context. How they do in the early hours, days and weeks will determine their outcome.'

Georgie looks absolutely shattered – all her efforts appear to be for naught. We stare at each other open-mouthed. There really aren't any words of comfort I can find.

We have given up hope of this being a short-term visit to the hospital. We now know that if we do leave here soon, we will either have two new seriously ill babies or we will leave on our own, as a devastated couple.

*

Our fears are confirmed the following day.

'J, can you come in here please?' Georgie is in the shower, her voice is cracked with fright.

I draw back the shower curtain. She stands shaking, bowed, her skinny naked frame and unfamiliar, still-round belly cocked forwards. And then the blood. Oh God, the blood.

It reminds me of the shower scene in *Psycho* – the bit Hitchcock doesn't show you after the guy comes with the knife . . . the bit he decided to leave to your imagination.

I stand, gawping, useless.

'Can you help me get out?' she says, stumbling. I jump up and put a towel around her and another between her legs and I help her across to the bed.

She sits down on the bed and then lies back and lets out a howl of desperation. She begins sobbing, her body bursting with emotion now that she knows that she has done everything she can.

'It's over, J,' she sobs.

Within minutes, a nurse is with us and minutes after that our obstetrician arrives. He has been on holiday in the Alps during the past week and I have to say it's a big relief to see him here now at this critical juncture. He reviews the scene and then turns to me. 'Can I talk to you outside, James?' he asks, and we turn out into the corridor.

He says, 'You have a difficult decision to make. The twins' chances of surviving at this juncture are, as you know, very slim.'

I nod.

'By the same token, Georgie has been in labour now for four days. You can see the impact it's having on her. I need to tell you that I am worried for her.'

He continues, 'I know you've been through a lot to get pregnant in the first place. And of course I understand the pressures you've been through as a couple to achieve a successful pregnancy. But you must realise that Georgie is now in serious danger. I am worried about her safety if we don't bring the twins out soon.'

It feels like something huge is coming. I realise with dread that there's absolutely nothing I can do about it. The sense of powerlessness is deeply troubling for someone like me, who likes to be in control at all times. I feel bounced like a pinball, my eyes constantly sting and the lump in my throat has taken up permanent residence. I'm one wrong turn away from losing it. It feels like we are hurtling towards disaster, but what shape that disaster will take is anyone's guess.

Because of Silky's statistics, I have started to prepare myself for the possibility that we might have to leave the hospital without our babies, but I'm not ready to leave the hospital alone.

The decision seems very straightforward to me. 'Let's do it,' I say.

'Good,' he says. 'I know it's difficult, but I think that's the right decision.'

5. Day 0

Within two hours of the twins' delivery, my parents arrive at the hospital.

My stomach is knotted with a combination of joy, shame and abject disappointment. I have longed for this moment, anticipating how proud I would feel introducing them to my babies for the first time and seeing Mum and Dad's beaming faces as they hold their new grandchildren.

My mind goes back to a recent photo of my Dad with my brother's newborn son Oliver. Dad's face is a picture of pride and delight and ever since seeing it I have wanted to put that same look onto my father's face, to make him truly proud of me.

'Everyone's alive,' I say, and they are beaming. I am so thankful that they are here to celebrate the victory of that statement.

A passing nurse says 'congratulations' and the tears start to prick my eyes. I save myself by launching into a garbled update of the evening's events.

'A boy and a girl – how cool is that? The boy came out first – he's been called "Twin 1, Boy" – at 8.56 p.m. and his sister "Twin 2, Girl" arrived a minute later at 8.57 p.m. Sorry about the names, we weren't expecting them until Christmas, so we haven't even bought a book of names yet. Anyway, Twin 1, Boy scored 9/10 on his Apgar test and Twin 2 scored 10/10 on hers. These are the tests they run on newborns to tell you how they're performing right at the outset. Twin 1, Boy weighed 670 grams, Twin 2, Girl weighed 660 grams. Pretty good start, isn't it?'

Mum's face falls. 'How much did you say they weighed?' she interjects, flustered.

'About 670 grams. Er, I think it's about a pound and a half.'

She looks ashen, but bravely summons a weak smile. 'Well done, James darling. We're so proud.'

'Your mother's made you some fish pie,' says Dad.

*

That night there are no phone calls to make from the hospital car park, no triumphant late-night messages to friends and family. No sense of victory, just a mixture of utter exhaustion, relief and, heaviest of all, dread about what will happen next.

6. Day 1

Early the next morning, we visit the twins in their new home in NICU, the neonatal intensive care unit. While Georgie recuperates from the surgery, we have set up camp in the maternity ward near to the neonatal unit – Georgie in the hospital bed and me on a temporary camp bed alongside on the floor. Neither of us has slept a wink.

We enter the NICU and are shown to the twins' cots.

What we see will never leave me.

Our tiny, tiny babies, barely identifiable as human beings, lie motionless in the centre of their incubators. They measure less than ten inches head to toe, their skin is a deep pink, almost translucent in appearance and covered in a light downy hair. Their bodies and limbs sprout from the tiniest of nappies which dwarf the trunks of their bodies. I notice the word 'Huggies' on the front of the nappies and feel slightly reassured. If Huggies makes nappies this small they must make a lot of them for it to be commercially viable – maybe our babies aren't so unusual after all.

No nipples! My god, why haven't they got nipples? Quite normal at this stage apparently, and everything else is perfect and just as it should be. A tiny button nose, a little pointy chin, ten minuscule fingers, ten minuscule toes – how amazing! Their legs are thinner and shorter than my little fingers. Their limbs, the muscles as yet unformed, lie floppy at their sides, giving them the appearance of frogs in shape and size.

Their eyes are still sealed shut and their mouths are stuffed with ventilator pipes.

Huge metal structures stand against the walls behind their incubators, designed to house the computer screens that track the babies' progress. A recurring dream strikes me – the one where I'm the pilot of a jumbo jet and I have to land the plane and I don't have a clue what all the screens and dials mean. A nurse called Ernie, whose serious face and tone mask the boisterous, happy nature which we will come to know so well, explains everything to us.

'Here on this screen,' she tells us, 'the green line monitors their heartbeats – you want it between a hundred and a hundred and seventy beats per minute. Blue is their oxygen saturation, the percentage of oxygen in the blood stream – you need to see that staying above ninety-five per cent ideally. Breaths per minute are the white line – we like to see around forty to sixty. They're doing fine.

'This frame here holds the drugs that are currently running into their bodies through their intravenous lines.'

It's a battery of syringes, I count six different hypodermics.

'So, we've got morphine, midazolam, vecuronium,

pancuronium, fluids and a few other bits and bobs. They manage the pain and also help to keep the babies semi-conscious to prevent them from fighting the ventilators and us nurses when we're trying to help them. They're running down through these intravenous lines here. One runs directly into the body by the arm here and these ones run into their arms and legs.' She points to the tiny tubes.

'We also keep the ventilation machine and the spare oxygen support for emergencies up here. And here is another screen which monitors the ventilator's settings, breaths per minute, oxygen levels, respiratory pressure and so on.'

We look at her expectantly.

'And that's everything.' She smiles.

Amid all the machinery, the pipes and metal bars, the screens and needles and bleeps, my eyes finally rest on the gauze bonnets which hold the ventilation pipes in place. Along the front of each bonnet, the nurses have lovingly placed stickers of ladybirds and bunny rabbits. These little baby motifs seem strangely out of place, but they are the only symbols in the whole room to remind us that this is a nursery for babies.

We are going to have to buy some teddies.

*

It is early evening on day 1, and Georgie and I sit with our twins. We are learning the ropes here and quickly starting to understand that the best we can do is to sit alongside our babies and whisper words of encouragement to them through the incubator doors.

Suddenly, BANG! The lights go out.

Not just in their room, not just in the hospital, but across a large swath of the south-east of England.

'Power cut!' a distant voice hollers.

There is a flurry of activity and we feel the energy in the room change from one of calm control to sudden panic. The banks of machinery – just moments before chugging along merrily with their green, red and blue flashing lights – suddenly shut down. We know our babies are being kept alive by the machines in the ward. And we know the machines are being kept alive by the power from the grid.

Shouts from the corridor, 'Everybody stay put and don't panic, the generator will kick in any second.' In the dim evening light I look across at Georgie and I can see her fear as well. The little screens are lifeless, the ventilators stilled, the room eerily silent all of a sudden.

The nurses jump to their routines. Stationing themselves between two incubators, they hold breathing bags over the mouths of the babies and each hand pumps frenetically to the right and to the left as they squeeze life-giving air into their charges.

Minutes elapse. Still nothing.

'Generator's failed,' comes a stage whisper from the corridor. We look on, more helpless than ever, but with an increasing sense of awe as we watch the nurses instinctively clicking into their drills to save the lives of every child in the Unit, including our two, tiny twins. For half an hour they stand pumping away while they wait for the engineers to fix the generator.

It will be morning before the power cut is resolved, but for now, in this critical corner of London, the engineers have overcome, the lights are back on and the ventilators are whirring their reassuring breaths again. Order has been resumed and stability returns to the ward.

Despite the drama, the twins are steady so Georgie and I agree that I should go and have a brief break – dinner with Mum and Dad at their flat nearby. I feel selfish, but I'm keen to keep myself emotionally charged through this period so I can support Georgie. She is still in a wheelchair and won't be allowed out of the hospital for several days yet. Not that she wants to leave . . .

*

I knock on the door of my parents' flat. Dad opens the door and folds me into a bear hug, instantly putting me in a stronger frame of mind. A glass of wine is thrust into my hand and within seconds I feel almost human again as the sofa envelops me and I launch into regaling my parents with the events of the past few hours.

They stand sipping their wine and their eyebrows sit high on their foreheads in the flickering candlelight as they listen to the dramatic events of the previous few hours.

My phone trills sharply in my pocket, shattering the sense of bonhomie. It's Georgie.

'J, our little girl is in trouble. She's had a heart attack. They told me to tell you to come quickly.'

'Oh God,' I reply. 'Coming right away.'

I stand to leave. 'Sorry . . . our little girl . . . doesn't sound good,' are the only words I say to my parents as I run out of the flat. From the sixth-floor flat I run down the stairs, stumbling in the dark, crashing into the walls as I turn each corner.

Panting, I reach street level where an eerie Dickensian scene greets me. The power grid is still down, the streetlamps are black and the roads have been plunged into darkness. The only light is from the sweeping headlights of cars passing along the road.

I flag desperately at passing taxis but they whizz by, oblivious to my pleading. All the taxis' lights are off, even those without passengers. What's going on? Is this some sort of conspiracy? Another empty taxi approaches and I step out into the middle of the road, hands clenched in supplication.

The car brakes sharply to avoid hitting me.

'Are you fucking mental? You trying to get yourself killed?' the cabbie shouts.

'I'm sorry. I need to get to the hospital.' I say. 'My baby daughter's just had a heart attack.'

'Hop in, mate. Let's go.'

'Thank you,' I say and jump aboard. We drive off down the dark streets, along the Mall and past Buckingham Palace, peculiarly sombre without its lit façade. I perch anxiously on the edge of the seat, willing the taxi to speed up. In the pit of my stomach, there's a growling fear about what I'm going to find when I get there. The chances of the twins surviving seem so slim and I have spent almost all of the past twenty-four hours considering how best to meet that situation when it arises. I have coached myself to remain calm; this is just nature taking its course, our twins should never have come so soon. They can't possibly survive, this is for the best. My concern has to be for Georgie and my attention must be focused on catching her when the inevitable happens. And yet that feels wrong somehow. This is my offspring, my lineage, my child. She may not yet have a first name, but she carries my family name – 'Melville-Ross: Twin 2, Girl'.

DAY 1

We're at the hospital in a few short minutes but the lifts are still down so I run up the stairs to the sixth floor. I arrive and someone points me towards the unit's 'quiet room' – reserved for serious discussions with parents – and I barge in sweaty and anxious about what I might find.

One of the consultants is seated in the gloom, explaining to Georgie, 'Your little girl has just had a major haemorrhage and she was a whisker away from dying. She has had a cardiac arrest and relapsed on four separate occasions.'

'Oh shit,' I say, helpfully.

'Normally we only give two shots of adrenalin to revive the babies before we give up. But on this occasion, the duty registrar felt sufficiently confident in your baby's spirit that she gave her four adrenalin shots. She went outside the usual operating procedure, but the decision has saved your baby's life.'

We blink our understanding like rabbits in the headlights. Our tiny brains struggle to imagine the torment that our baby has just been through. I can't help but think of the scene in *Pulp Fiction* when John Travolta administers the adrenalin shot to Uma Thurman's heart. That just happened to our little girl. Four times.

I try not to imagine the scene around her incubator in the last hour.

*

It's late, our daughter is stable now and so we decide to turn in. It's been quite a day.

Georgie remains stone-faced despite these trials. She seems to be in shock. Inwardly I'm sure that she, like me, must be terrified that they might die. But unlike me, she refuses to mention it or even consider it. She urges them to survive as if she can make that happen through the sheer force of her will. They must make it! They have to!

I, for myself, can't bring myself to discuss with her how I feel for fear of letting the side down. The truth is I feel utterly deflated by what has happened in the past week. My life's ambition has always been to become a dad and for years it had looked as though it might never happen. Now it has and it's nothing like my dreams. I've been a parent for little more than twenty-four hours and I can't say I'm hugely enthusiastic about the experience so far.

The camp bed squeaks as I roll over to face the wall and try to sleep.

I cast my mind back to the magpies in the park.

One for sorrow . . .

7. Day 2

While I focus on the twins and Georgie, my mother, father, brother and sister are all focused on me. We have always been a close-knit group, but now that sense of belonging increases as we circle the wagons and square up to the biggest challenge we have ever faced as a collective. They know that the snatched moments outside the hospital – a brief respite for a walk or coffee – are the oxygen that keep me going, keep me strong, away from the dramas in the hospital. I'm reluctant to leave Georgie or the twins for even a second, but realise there's sense in taking short breaks.

Two days after the twins' arrival, Mum and I take a walk through St James's Park. It's been a long, hot August and the late summer sun glistens on the water of the lake. The fairy-tale towers above Horse Guards Parade speak of fortitude and fantastic dreams. The contrast with our conversation is palpable as we try to make sense of the emotional bombardment we are all facing.

'I'm really worried about Georgie,' I say and Mum protectively loops her arm through mine as we walk. 'She seems dedicated to the point of obsession and I just worry what will happen if they don't make it.'

'How do you feel about it?' she asks.

'I'm just being realistic. We know they only have a one-in-five chance, and after last night I just don't see how they will survive.'

'You have to believe that they will, darling,' she says.

A small group of Canada geese struts past, honking.

'I desperately want that to be the case, but I can't see past the statistics. I just need to focus on Georgie,' I say. 'She's going to fall so hard when they die. She's totally convinced that they are going to make it and is throwing herself into the emotional care of the twins.'

We stop and I turn to face her.

'But I just can't get beyond the facts. They're either going to die or be disabled. And I honestly don't think I could cope if they were disabled,' I confess. 'I think I'd rather they didn't make it.'

I feel dreadful saying it, but it's out now: This huge, awful truth that will come to haunt me in the years to come.

'Let's just take each day as it comes, James,' says Mum.

'I do so long for them to make it, Mum,' I say, back-pedalling. 'I want nothing more. But all the dreams, the wishes for the future – the hopes that they'll one day be holding down high-powered jobs that make me proud – none of that matters any more.'

DAY 2

'They're making you proud already, James, just by the very fact of their survival,' she says. 'Be happy for that.'

We stand on the bridge and huddled together we offer up our own silent prayers for the twins and for Georgie.

God has not been a particular feature of my life to this point, but he is about to make his presence felt in a very significant way.

8. Day 3

'You need to come quickly; it's your boy. I'm afraid it is bad.'
The words are unnecessary. Just the look on the nurse's
face is enough to tell us it's serious.

Here we go again.

We follow silently through the empty, late-night corridors,
our minds racing with questions but too aware that the nurse
sent to fetch us is not the one whose job it is to properly answer
them.

Camilla, the consultant in charge that night, is that person;
her face wears a stern appearance as she greets us. She stands
between us and the incubator as we enter the ward and she
starts to fill us in.

'He has had a major pulmonary haemorrhage. His lungs
are filled with blood so he's not getting any oxygen around his
body. He has been like this now for twenty minutes.'

She steps aside and our eyes fall to our son. He is lying flat out, arms and legs akimbo, his body completely lifeless. His colour has turned from the deep pink of the past few days to a pale grey. He is totally motionless, save for the ventilator machine-gunning breaths of air into his body. The visual effect is extraordinary: a tiny limp, lifeless body, throbbing to the beat of the oscillator, which is desperately fighting to save his life.

Camilla explains the scene. 'We've paralysed him with sedative to stop him from fighting against our efforts to save him. The ventilation machine has been switched to a special setting to get as much oxygen into his lungs as possible and to try to keep them open. If we have the ventilator on a normal setting, there's a risk the lungs get stuck closed when he breathes out and we may not get them open again.'

'The reason for his colour is that he is not getting any oxygenated blood around his system. If you look at the saturation monitor, which tells us how much oxygen he has passing around his body, you can see it's very low.'

The number on the screen is 15 per cent. I remember Ernie's tutorial on day 1. It should be over 95 per cent.

A nurse is taking photographs. For the first time, they have put a tiny blanket over him and dressed him in a tiny bodysuit. We know enough to know that this gesture is purely presentational . . . there is no medical benefit to him being clothed in the warm cocoon of the incubator. We watch the nurse, her head bowed sympathetically, and we realise, if we didn't before, that this is serious.

Suddenly his oxygen levels plummet, this time to 4 per cent. Georgie slumps into the chair that has been brought up and reaches into the incubator to stroke her son.

She gasps. 'He's so cold.'

And there it is again, that fearful sense deep in my stomach that the end is imminent – the moment at which the attention will turn to me to catch Georgie, the moment at which I will be truly tested.

Camilla too seems to have made her mind up. A deep sigh before she opens her mouth.

'Mum. Dad. It's not good, I'm afraid.' She pauses as if girding herself for what she has to say next and then, with a jarring certainty in her voice, 'Your baby is going to die.'

Silence.

'Do you want to have him baptised?'

Nothing.

Eventually we look at each other and we nod like automatons. Disbelieving, speechless, powerless.

'Have him baptised,' she continues, 'and once that's done we'll disconnect him from the ventilator and let you take him into the quiet room to hold him while he passes away.'

We stand numbed by the horror in front of us and the agony of seeing our own child suffering such trauma.

I have never seen anyone die before and now I am going to have to go through this experience for the first time with my own son. No one should have to bury their own child, let alone see them die in their arms. One image keeps returning to my mind – a vision of me carrying a tiny coffin through a churchyard.

My head and eyes are swimming as I glance up at the clock. It is past midnight. It is my birthday.

*

DAY 3

On the morning of the previous day, as we sat alongside our twins' incubators, Georgie said, 'We need to decide on names.' Leafing through the book of names presented a happy distraction. We giggled guiltily at some of the more outlandish names, but soon landed on Thomas Alexander for our boy and Alice Lara for our little girl.

Because Georgie's sister Alice has been a constant presence and a huge support during the past few traumatic days, we wanted to mark her contribution – the love she has shown and liberal hugs she has doled out – in this way. She made the mistake of looking through the window of the operating theatre as the twins were delivered and I'm not sure that her first sight of her namesake will leave her any time soon.

Thomas takes his name from his great-great-grandfather – an American born at the end of the nineteenth century who had been a pilot, a gold prospector and a professional wrestler. Our hope was that some of his spirit would rub off on our son and, considering this thought, I was momentarily transported back to my childhood.

I am sitting with my father's father, Groni, in the living room in his house in Sussex, and listening to him regale me with tales about his own father.

'You know he was a pilot in the Great War?' says Groni.

'Yes!' I exclaim proudly. 'He was a mersary!'

Groni chuckles. 'That's right, a mercenary. Do you know, he was the fourth person in the United States to have a pilot's licence? I've still got it in my desk somewhere. Do you want to see it?' he says, unfolding his large, still-athletic frame from his armchair and crossing to the desk in the corner of the room.

'Here it is!' he says, recovering the small, dog-eared piece of card from his desk drawer.

'Wow!' I say, as he passes it to me. And there on the faded yellow card, is a picture of my great-grandfather beneath the title: 'United States of America, Department of Commerce, Office of the Director of Aeronautics'. And alongside the words 'Pilot's License No.' is the number 0000004.

'He used to hire himself out around the world to whoever would pay him the most,' my grandfather continues talking as I turn the card over in my hand. 'He flew for Pancho Villa and the rebels in the Mexican Revolution, he was involved in the Russo-Japanese War of 1905 and then finally he flew for the French in the First World War, which is how we all came to be British.'

'How's that, Groni?' I ask.

He reaches for a cigarette, puts it to his lips and snaps a lighter open. Then he continues, the unlit cigarette waggling between his lips as he speaks. 'Well, planes in those days weren't terribly robust and moved pretty slowly so you were something of a sitting duck to anyone who wanted to have a pot at you. He got shot down a lot as a pilot, but on the final occasion he was badly injured and sent to Britain to recover. This is where he met and fell in love with your great-grandmother – Katherine Mount, my mother. She was the nurse who put him back together again.'

He sparks the lighter and inhales deeply, enjoying the smoke rushing into his mouth and then spilling out into the room. I fidget impatiently for the next chapter of his story.

'She was a tall girl, six foot, and she fell in love with him while she nursed him back to health.' He continues. 'He was still prone when he proposed from his bed and she accepted before she realised just how short he was . . . He was only five-foot-six! I think she was a bit disappointed when he finally stood on his feet for the marriage ceremony! Ha! We all get our height from her, not Thomas, you see?'

I nod, smiling, captivated. It's true, we are all tall. Groni well over six foot, and my Dad stands at six-foot-six. Already my brother and I are starting to sprout – he has recently been through three shoe sizes in one term.

'But he was immensely strong,' he continues. 'Stand up!' he commands and I leap to my feet.

He takes me by my belt buckle and lifts me with one arm, up against the wall.

'Even when your grandfather was in his seventies, he could still lift me up like this. Did you know he was a professional wrestler?'

'Yes,' I reply, from my unusual vantage point. The ceilings in my grandfather's living room are not high and I'm crunched into the corner of ceiling and wall.

'During his wrestling career he billed as "The Pocket Rocket" on account of his size. Fantastically strong wrists – square block wrists they call them – thicker in depth than across,' he grasps his holding wrist to demonstrate, shuffling me further into the corner of wall and ceiling. My head bangs against the ceiling as he does so. The smoke from the cigarette in his mouth is spilling up into my eyes.

'Er, can I get down now, Groni?' I splutter.

'Yes, of course.' He replies, suddenly aware of the peculiar nature of the situation. We sit back down and Groni continues the story.

'Then there was the gold prospecting. Haha! Funny story . . . He set off alone into Alaska, with nothing but a sledge and a pack of huskies, looking to find gold and make his fortune. Now, as you can imagine, food was pretty scarce up there on the frozen wastes, so the trick was to chuck a stick of dynamite out onto a frozen lake and the explosion would blow a hole in the ice, stun the fish and they would float up to the surface. Hey presto, dinner!'

'That's genius!' I say.

'Yes indeed,' he continues. 'However, on this one occasion, your great-grandfather proved that all geniuses have their moments of stupidity. Oh dear. He failed to tether all of the huskies to the sledge and one of them went haring off after the dynamite, thinking this was a game of fetch! Haha! The dog retrieved the stick of dynamite and came running back towards Thomas, who himself, turned and started running as fast as he could in the opposite direction!'

'Oh no!' I say. 'What happened?'

'Well, you know it's not true that Roger Bannister ran the first four-minute mile . . .' he says, pausing for the punchline. 'Your great-grandfather did it in the early twentieth century in Alaska! Wearing snowshoes!'

We burst into peals of laughter.

'Pity about the dog!' he shouts as I roll on the sofa, giggling.

*

A priest has arrived at Thomas's incubator. In his dog collar, he looks out of place in this medical setting. He wears an appropriately serious expression and introduces himself as John.

He wheels the small trolley that the nurses use for measuring out drugs up to the side of Thomas's incubator. He lays a white cloth over the trolley to create his makeshift altar and places a small silver cross and bowl in the middle.

The service lasts no longer than a minute.

John draws the sign of the cross on Thomas's tiny, grey forehead with water from the bowl and mutters some prayers which we dutifully Amen.

Now my heart fills my throat as I realise that the Amen signals the end of the service. It is the signal for Thomas to be disconnected from his life support.

We say our solemn goodbyes, I kiss my finger and reach into the incubator to pass the kiss to his forehead. I realise that I had never got to feel my kiss on his skin, never even held him before now. And now I will hold him at last, just as he breathes his last breath. As I say my goodbye to someone I've known for all of 72 hours it strikes me how much I never want to be without him.

It is over. There is nothing left to do. The moment has come for him to be disconnected and for his short, miserable existence to be ended. Peace for him after three turbulent days of battle.

*

And then it happens. Something utterly unexpected. I don't think it's hyperbole to call it a miracle.

Slowly but surely, the level of Thomas's oxygen saturation starts to climb back up. The little blue number that had become so significant in the past few minutes flickers through the teens, slowly at first and then with gathering momentum as it accelerates through the twenties and thirties, skipping numbers on the way. The bemused nurses and doctors are stirred into action, glancing at one another with surprise as Thomas comes back to life.

I look round to find the priest who had prevailed where logic and medicine had conceded defeat, but he has left the ward, left the unit and left our lives forever.

We step back from the incubator and are ushered out and into the unit's quiet room.

Suddenly our previously mute mouths are full of questions for each other. Dare we hope? Did that really just happen? Is he going to be OK? Perhaps invoking the name of his extraordinary ancestor has stirred some fresh determination to survive.

A few minutes later, Camilla joins us.

'I have never seen anything like that. Amazing.' She seems lost for words.

'I can't understand it but we have him back to a steady state. He's stable. You need to understand that he's still highly vulnerable, but we have him back to where we wanted him. There's nothing more to do tonight so go to bed and we'll wake you if anything happens overnight. I can't promise he'll make it through the night, but he's safe for now.'

'Can we say goodnight to him?' Georgie asks.

'Of course.'

It's now 2 a.m. and we return to Thomas and pass a kiss on our fingers through the doors of the incubator. Already the pink has returned to his previously grey skin. We look at one another and marvel at the suddenness of his turnaround.

We return to our room, settle into our beds and switch the light off. We lie in next-door beds, still as stones, staring unblinking at the ceiling, too shocked by the evening's events to speak to each other and unable to sleep for listening out for footsteps in the corridor and a knock at our door.

Thomas will survive the night. By the morning he will be back to where he began the previous day – in a stable but highly fragile state.

9. Day 4

B al Sharma, one of the senior consultants on the unit wants to talk to us. He settles into the chair in the corner of our room with the air of someone who looks like he has something important to announce. He has a kind face and his words bring reassuring warmth, carried on a melodious rhythm.

'A difficult night, isn't it?' he begins.

'Yes,' we agree. 'Frightening.'

'Yes. As you know, Thomas came very close to losing his life last night. We need to discuss what we do if that happens again.'

'OK.' We nod, nervous about what he's about to say.

'Thomas spent a considerable length of time without decent levels of oxygen last night. It's reasonable to assume that his brain will have sustained some sort of injury during that period. If it happens again, we really need to think about whether it is in Thomas's – and indeed your – best interests to revive him.'

I shoot a nervous glance at Georgie, but her eyes are focused on the doctor.

'In such circumstances death is sometimes not necessarily the worst outcome.'

He pauses. Now comes the hard bit.

'I need to ask you an important question,' he continues softly.

We lean in to hear, even though we are pretty sure we know what's coming.

'I need to ask your permission *not* to resuscitate Thomas if such an event recurs,' he says.

What a desperate situation. Less than a week ago we had been looking forward to a life as a family of four. And now, for the second time in a week, I feel totally powerless in the face of nature's unalterable course.

And yet, isn't what we are doing completely counter to nature's way? The babies are being kept alive via means that nature had never intended to allow – our doctors are playing God. Somewhere it strikes me that all this is wrong. That the doctors are only extending an agony that could have been prevented if only they'd been allowed to die at the start.

But now that I am presented with the choice, now that it comes down to this critical, awful decision, deep down I realise that I want them to survive, I want that so badly.

So what's it to be? What a question for three-day-old parents to have to answer! On the one hand, if we insist on keeping Thomas alive, would the damage done to his brain make his life an utterly pointless existence? On the other, if we give permission to switch the ventilator off, are we denying him the chance to at least try to prove himself? Given how hard he had battled the previous night, surely he had done enough to prove that he could make a go of it? I feel hopelessly untrained to cope with a question this complicated, this profound.

Time for a breather . . . we need time to consider this dilemma. After the events of last night, and having nearly missed the opportunity on the first night, we decide to have Alice baptised as well.

Soon afterwards, Georgie is feeling faint and in pain again so she goes back to the room. I decide to go for a walk outside to ponder our decision, so I march down the entrance way to the hospital and down along the South Bank. I stand looking across the river to the Victoria Embankment on the opposite side of the river. The London Eye is at my back, the Houses of Parliament and Big Ben beyond Westminster Bridge to my left, and Cleopatra's Needle away to my right. My monumental problem suddenly seems very small in the context of this grandeur and history.

A flashback to twenty years earlier, the first time I had seen these sights from the back seat of my parents' car. I was squeezed against the window by my brother and sister as we strained to see the sights our parents were explaining to us. The obelisk of Cleopatra's Needle was the one thing that stuck in my mind from that first visit to the capital. This huge ancient stone structure reaching up to the sky – speaking of distant, unfamiliar lands and so alien in its modern London surroundings.

I call my father to ask his advice about Dr Sharma's question. Dad, my idol. Six-foot-six of authority, composure, common sense and calm. The man with all the answers . . .

'I can't answer that,' he says.

Shit, this is serious, I think to myself. Dad's never not had the answer. But I realise it's a deeply unfair question to put to him. Suddenly I realise he's human after all and these questions are no more easily answered by him than they are by me. I realise it's time for me to grow up, time for me to stand on my own two feet. These decisions aren't taken by committee, Georgie and I must make the biggest decision of our lives.

Back at the hospital, Georgie and I sit side by side on her bed, contemplating this terrible question.

'We need a crystal ball to see into the future,' I state glumly.

'How can we possibly tell what the outcome will be?' Georgie asks angrily.

'Impossible,' I agree.

'Poor Thomas,' she says and it feels strange to hear her use his name for the first time. Stranger still that she may only use it a handful more times. Strange that she may never use it to call him in from the garden, to admonish him for bad behaviour or to tell him how proud she is of him.

'Perhaps he's suffered enough,' I proffer as a starting point . . .

*

We take some time to deliberate during the remainder of the day and later we catch up with Bal Sharma again.

I say, 'Your guidance seems pretty clear. We are worried about the quality of life that Thomas will suffer if he sustains another event like last night.' He nods and I continue, 'We don't want you to resuscitate him if he goes through a similar event again.'

I can't believe the words are coming out of my mouth. After his victory last night it feels like a betrayal. Thomas has proved his mettle, but we are living in fantasy land if we think he is going to survive many more events like that.

Georgie bursts into tears beside me. I put my arm around her shoulders and pull a tissue from the box on the table in the middle of the room. I pass it to her and she buries her face in her hands, tissue and all. It's the hardest decision we have ever had to make. We are stunned with shock and exhaustion.

Bal replies, 'I realise how difficult that is. We see some of the children later in life and you need to understand that life is very hard for them and for their families. It's the right call.'

Suddenly the prospect of severe disability looms into view and I realise what he means. 'You may feel powerless in all of this right now. You may feel like it's all down to the medical staff,' Bal says. 'But you need to realise that your job is the most important one. Be with your babies, talk to them, sing to them, let them know how much you love them. They are listening and they grow stronger every hour with your support.'

10. Day 5

I'm worried about Georgie.

To be honest, I haven't seen the real her for the last ten days. She has been the focus of my attention throughout that time, but all my efforts to rally her and keep her going have been fruitless.

She's listless, emotionally and physically, seemingly shell-shocked by the events of the past ten days. I remind myself of the trauma she has undergone – the haemorrhaging, five days of labour, the caesarean and now debilitating migraines which make it impossible for her to get out of bed some mornings. Five days after the birth she is still in a wheelchair. It's a lot for a body to go through, even before you get into the psychological battles we've both had to face with the regular barrage of near-death experiences for our twins.

We sit in our room; the scene is part hospital room, part flower shop. There isn't a shelf space left which isn't covered by beautiful bouquets of flowers, cards or baskets of cakes. We are truly blessed to have so many friends and family rooting for us but they feel so far away now. And I know they feel the same, powerless to support us in our hour of need.

Georgie and I perch alongside each other on the bed, plates on our laps, pushing food around but unable to face the act of eating. We don't talk much; neither of us knows what to say. Neither of us has the ability to say the right thing: the one thing that will make everything all right.

'It's going to be OK,' I keep reassuring her, but the words ring hollow.

At night time we sit by the twins' incubators – evenings extending into night and then night stretching to dawn as the twins battle another few hours further into their lives.

When we do make it to bed, we lie side by side staring through the dark at the lights on the ceiling. I reach up from my bed on the floor to her in the hospital bed above me. I squeeze her hand. She squeezes mine, but there's no purpose behind it.

Husband and wife. Father and mother. Lovers and best friends. But miles apart buffeted off our normal course by the events of the past few days. We're both exhausted. It is impossible to see where the next let-up will come from.

But come it does, the following morning, in the robust form of our midwife, Marjorie.

Bang! The door swings open and crashes into a chair.

'Right!' She barks in her strong Northern accent. 'Come on you, out of bed.'

The two of us peek out from underneath our hospital sheets. What the fuck? We're not expecting this. We've been so used to people tiptoeing around us these past few days.

And then the riot act is read to us in no uncertain terms.

'No lounging about in bed today. No wheelchair, you're

walking everywhere today. You're not allowed back in this room until lunchtime and then only for a half-hour.'

'Go on, you too!' she said, kicking me in my temporary bed on the floor.

The imposing figure stands, hands on hips, looming over my bed. I'm not arguing.

I scramble to my feet, stung by the implication that we're not coping, but privately acknowledging that this is just what's needed to get some momentum into us.

'Your babies need you to be strong, go and be with them. Talk to them and tell them you love them!'

*

Two days later and finally Georgie is well enough to go home, to our house in Tooting. Marjorie's intervention has provided a much-needed impetus and I'm relieved that we will finally be returning home, relieved that Georgie is well enough to leave the medical support behind. It's a sure sign that we are making progress on one front at least.

It's evening and Mum and Dad have arrived at the hospital to bring us home. I'm buoyed by this symbolic moment but Georgie's thoughts seem to be elsewhere. As we walk out of the hospital into the car park, Georgie steps into the low, summer-evening sun and blinks like a prisoner released from captivity.

The four of us load the car with all the clobber that we have acquired over the past week – our overnight bags, tins of cakes, un-read and, for the moment irrelevant, parenting books, medicines for Georgie and the now-bedraggled flowers which have survived the week in our hot room. It feels like something is missing.

The London traffic is not kind to us. There is a gridlock on Tooting High Street. The bright street lights and car tail lights shed an array of colour onto the faces and multi-coloured saris of the shoppers on the pavement. A corner grocery store is a bustle of business as everyone goes about their daily lives.

Georgie stares blankly out of the window, her face lit by the intermittent stop-start of the brake lights of the traffic ahead of us.

'Can you remember the short cut, George?' I ask.

Her mind is elsewhere.

'I think it's here, Dad. Try a right here,' I say.

We turn right into a cul-de-sac. 'Shit, sorry. About turn.'

It's another forty-five minutes before we get home to our little two-up two-down terraced house.

Georgie goes into the house while I unpack the car with Mum and Dad. Once everything has been brought in, I go to find her. She is sitting, shoulders slumped, on the bed in the spare room: the spare room that doesn't even have cots in it yet, no baby wallpaper or curtains. The reason for her distance starts to dawn on me.

I sit down next to her on the bed. 'All right, George?' She doesn't answer me.

I put my arm around her and she rests her head into my shoulder.

'Everything OK?' I try again.

Downstairs Mum and Dad are fussing in the kitchen, starting to prepare the evening meal.

'They should be with us,' she says suddenly.

I now realise what a big deal this will have been for her, to leave the hospital without the twins. I'd viewed this homecoming as a huge step forward but for Georgie, the agony of abandonment is now writ large across her exhausted face. As I look around the room, I realise that this house offers nothing in the way of comfort for her. Its meaning has changed forever.

She looks out to the garden. It is a beautiful late summer's evening. 'I just feel so empty,' she says. 'All the dreams of playing in the garden with them – am I going to get that chance? It's all wrong.'

I squeeze her shoulders.

'Why are we here?' she says suddenly. 'Why have we left them? We should be with them.'

*

I've been absent for a fortnight now, so it's time I returned to work. I work for a financial communications firm in the City, called Financial Dynamics. It is a busy and demanding job, the hours are long, but I love it and thankfully it is a big firm, so my workload has been covered by my wonderfully understanding team mates. My boss and team have been very supportive and have told me to take as much time as I need, but I'm keen to return.

I can tell from the looks on my colleagues' faces that many of them are lost for words when I return, even though they know so little of the events of the past week. Many more are oblivious and why shouldn't they be? But the return to normality is a great tonic for me and I'm soon settling in to the bustle and bonhomie of the office environment.

It's harder for Georgie, who spends her days at the hospital, still living the daily – hourly – rollercoaster of the twins' survival. In the evenings I walk into our living room and find her sitting on the sofa, just staring at the walls. The worry for the twins and the awful sense of maternal abandonment are taking a heavy toll.

In the shed at the bottom of our garden, there are unfinished picture frames that Georgie was working on when things first started to go wrong with the pregnancy. She has recently started her own picture-framing business called Pudding and Pie Frames. She had put her career as a freelance marketer on hold two years earlier when it became apparent that the stress of her busy job was a factor in preventing her from becoming pregnant. The framing business had allowed her to maintain her passion for creativity but in a low-stress environment.

I count my lucky stars that I married someone with the grit and determination to see through an episode like this.

Seven years ago, before we were married, Georgie and I had travelled to Hong Kong to find our fortunes. It was shortly before the territory was handed over to China, so opportunity and challenges abounded. We didn't find our fortunes, but we left with enough money to travel through the Far East and witness the breath-taking splendour of structures like Angkor in Cambodia and Borobudur in Indonesia.

But perhaps one of my favourite memories, and the one which cemented my view that I had to marry Georgie, was our ascent of Mount Merapi, an active volcano on Java. The plan was to rise at 3 a.m. and climb to the summit in order to enjoy the sunrise from the top. So we went to bed early to get some rest ahead of the ascent. What we hadn't bargained on was that the village we were staying in would shortly be celebrating the start of Eid, the Islamic festival to celebrate the end of the month's fasting during Ramadan. And so, just as we are nodding off at midnight, the muezzin lets rip with his celebratory call, blasted through the loudspeakers around the village. Half an hour later, his wailing is suddenly and unexpectedly accompanied by Snap's 'I Got the Power'.

And all the while, the muezzin's wail continues over the top. Neither sound is especially enriching, but combined, at one o'clock in the morning, the cacophony is unbearable. This unhappy state of affairs continues until the faint beep of our alarm clocks tells us that it's time to rise for our volcano climb.

We rise, dress and make our way to the allotted meeting point. We join a group of a dozen other travellers and our tour guide, whose gnarled features suggest that he is north of seventy. But soon enough, he is showing us a clean pair of heels as he scampers off into the dark and up the mountain path. The pitch-black path winds inexorably upwards and we follow him up, one behind the other along the narrow trail.

After a short while, the numbers in our group start to dwindle as more and more of the group begin to turn back. 'Too dark, too dangerous,' they call as they turn for home. Georgie's face wears a grim determination throughout. In the end, the group shrinks to a small handful of us who reach the rocky summit. It's just before dawn and the sight of the fiery glow of the lava sliding down from the summit is our reward for sticking to the task. Shortly, the sun starts to rise over the misty Javan mountain range.

I put my arm around Georgie as we stand shivering at the top, and think to myself, she's the one for me. While everyone else was dropping off and falling back from the task, she stuck to it. The glow of the sun starts to warm our faces and scatter the mist and it's time to turn back down the slope to the village.

11. September

I stand staring absent-mindedly through the large plate-glass window of the neonatal intensive care unit. The blistering hot summer is extending its reach into autumn and the hospital's front lawn maintains its yellow, dusty hue.

The twins have survived their first two weeks and the doctors have set December as a realistic target date for their homecoming, if – and it's still such a big 'if' – they survive. The unspoken rule is that we understand that they're talking generalities here, but it's a target to aim for, a distant mark on the far horizon to keep us holding onto the slim chance that they will make it.

Just as importantly, Georgie is also coming back to life. The physical strains of the previous few weeks are subsiding day by day and she strengthens as she steels herself now to the task of battling alongside the twins for their survival.

I look at the grass outside and start to imagine it regaining its colour as we approach Christmas. The rain will come, the grass will green and the leaves will fall. Who knows, by December we may even have snow on the lawn.

'She's ready now,' says one of the nurses.

I cross the room to Alice's incubator. It's a big day for us; a fortnight after their arrival, the moment has come when we will be allowed to touch our babies. Until now, any handling has required us to wear surgical, blue gloves. It hasn't been the most satisfactory way for new parents to try to form a physical bond with their newborns.

Georgie settles in to the chair by Alice's bed and reaches through the porthole. She gently opens the poppers on her Babygro and strokes her downy chest with her little finger. I watch her and feel a strong swell of love towards them both, also a sense of victory. This tiny action is such a huge step forward for all of us.

Next it's my turn. She feels warm and soft and I'm suddenly aware of my love building. I look at her face and recognise Georgie's distinctive nostrils for the first time and realise that Alice is the spit of her mother. We may not have created much – these scraps of human life – but we have created something and I am suddenly, for the first time, drawn to realise the love that I have for this child, these children.

'Time to go,' says Georgie after a while. I've lost the time, immersed in these wonderful, new feelings.

'Another day they've survived,' I say to Georgie as she comes up behind me. She squeezes my hand, three times – a longstanding custom of our relationship.

One, two, three.

I, love, you.

We both feel like we are being tested in new and not altogether pleasant ways, but we also know that we have each other and that we couldn't do this if we didn't. Now the benefit of the years spent as friends and partners through university, on our travels and in London comes to the fore. We instinctively know that our relationship is not something we need to worry about, that the twins may not survive this but our relationship will. It's not arrogance or presumptuousness, it just is, and that is our reward for all those years together.

In the car on the way home we chat about our day.

Georgie says, 'That was lovely being able to touch Alice today.'

'Today was a good day, wasn't it?' I smile. 'I feel I'm starting to make a bond now. I'm sorry I've been distant from the twins in these early weeks; I just didn't think they'd make it. I still worry that they won't and I just want to be there for you if the unthinkable happens.'

Georgie is silent.

'I guess you don't have the luxury of that distance. Sorry,' I say.

There's a pause, then I say, 'Nurse Laura was laughing at me today.'

'Why?' asks Georgie.

'Because I kept asking about the charts. I was like "What does this line mean? Why has this statistic dropped so suddenly in this particular hour? What do these letters stand for?" I was going on a bit; probably getting in her way, to be honest.'

'Why was she laughing?'

'Apparently all the dads do it. We all feel so useless that we immerse ourselves in the charts and technology so we feel we have a role to play. I think I'm being really clever by getting all the details, but I'm simply conforming to stereotype.'

'That's funny.'

'I know.'

A long silence.

'What's happening, J?' she says eventually.

'What do you mean?' I ask.

'I've got so many questions and we just don't seem to be getting any answers,' she says.

'What do you mean?' I ask again. I know what she means.

'Like: When do you think they will be stable? When will they be able to move out of intensive care into special care? When will they be able to breathe on their own? What's the long-term picture?'

'Yeah, I know. Big questions.' I say. 'Impossible.'

'Hmm, I know.'

'We just have to take each day as it comes.'

'Each hour,' she replies.

*

Over the coming weeks we unwittingly become medical experts. Medicine is not a subject that either of us understands well, but we soon find ourselves becoming well versed in the narrow field of neonatology.

Collapsed lungs – hitherto a situation that we would have felt was almost certainly terminal – become an almost daily occurrence and we become immune to the news of another incident.

I've learned to say 'necrotising enterocolitis' all by myself, which makes me feel very important and clever. This is a disease of the gut which Thomas has spent several days battling. Once again we're told to prepare for the worst, to prepare for the fact that he won't last the day. Once again Thomas puts up a brave rear-guard action and sees it off.

Infections become a regular feature as well. We were warned at the outset that they could potentially have a life-threatening impact on the twins and yet each time they fight to survive, sometimes in isolation units to avoid cross-infection. Thomas even manages to acquire a particularly virulent infection called *acinetobacter*, a superbug which has been brought back to the UK by soldiers who have been fighting in Iraq. For this indiscretion, he is put into a sealed room on his own and we are no longer allowed to touch him without rubber gloves. Perhaps he's arranged this bug deliberately, giving him, as it does, a nurse all to himself for twenty-four hours a day. Given the way that the nurses have taken him to their hearts, it's clear that he has been paying attention.

At work, people ask me how the twins are doing. Once or twice, to start with, I tell them the truth, that it's an hour-by-hour existence, that Thomas nearly lost his life again last night, but the conversation ends in awkwardness. So I dress it up and tell them that the twins are alive and getting stronger hour by hour. Life in the bubble of the hospital and back at work are poles apart and, for now, it will need to stay that way.

But here at the hospital, there's something very special, very unusual happening and we can tell from the way the medical staff are responding to these brave babies, just how extraordinary their survival story is, even for those who see these events every week.

*

One morning, at 4 a.m., the phone sounds shrilly by our bedside and we jerk awake.

'James, hi, it's Caroline from the hospital.' Caroline is one of our favourite nurses; her diminutive frame and mild manner belie her planet-sized heart.

'Hi Caroline, what's happened?' I reply groggily.

'It's Alice. She's not well. We need you guys to come in,' she replies.

'Thanks, we're on our way.'

We dress swiftly, in silence, and run to the car. We race the car through the empty London streets, eyes glazed by tiredness, but brains jumping with questions we'll have to wait to ask.

We arrive at the hospital and, despite the urgency, we plod through our routine as we arrive at NICU: press the buzzer . . . Nervous, fidgety seconds as we wait to be allowed in. Is anyone sitting at the desk, have they heard it ring, is anyone going to let us in? We're through.

Now wash hands. Thoroughly. I go to the right-hand sink, Georgie to the left. Wash hands with the same meticulous routine. Back of the hands, between fingers, each finger on each hand. Three pieces of paper towel – no more no less. Through onto the ward and a squirt of hand gel from the right-hand bottle, never the left-hand one. Have I got OCD? These superstitions are ridiculous, but they haven't failed me yet. The twins are still alive, aren't they?

'I'm so sorry for calling you,' says the consultant in charge. It's Tim, an austere, silver-haired Australian. We wave away his concerns. 'She's taken a bit of a dip and we're worried her little body might not be strong enough for the fight.'

'What's happened?' Georgie asks.

'She's got another infection and it has caused her oxygen requirement to shoot up,' he explains. 'As we pump more air into her tiny ribcage, so the heart is squashed, preventing it from pumping the necessary amounts of blood around the body. The brain then has to make a difficult decision about which organs require blood most urgently and prioritises the distribution of blood to the brain and lungs. The knock-on effect of this is that minor organs are overlooked and so, in some cases, we start to see organs like the kidneys start to pack up. That's what's happening now with Alice.'

We look on, worry on our tired faces.

'We're doing everything we can,' Tim says. 'I'm so sorry, it's down to Alice now but I think we need to be realistic about her chances. I'm afraid it doesn't look good.'

He pauses, seemingly unsure of how to convey the next sentence: they are words which he has no desire to say. Words, nonetheless, he knows it is his duty to convey.

'You need to prepare yourselves for the possibility that she might not win this one. She's obviously strong, but she's in a dangerous place at the moment.'

He flinches. The words seem to hurt him as much as us and he turns to leave.

We stand alongside Alice and I put my arm around Georgie. Her tears drop onto the roof of the incubator and she quickly wipes them away with the sleeve of her jumper.

We stay by Alice's side all morning, occasionally reaching in and stroking our daughter who has fought so hard to survive and who now needs to fight once again. We talk to her and occasionally sing to her. I wonder if she can hear us, we have to assume she can.

I put my head up close to the glass and make a solemn promise.

'My darling, you have to keep fighting. Your mother and father love you so much. You've got so much to look forward to if you do make it. You and your brother are going to have such a wonderful life. I'm going to work so hard every day to make sure you always have everything you need – the best home, the best school, the best life. It's going to be such fun, but I need you to fight again. Just one more time, fight for your life, for all it's worth. I promise you the battle will be worth it. I'll make sure of it.'

*

It's now 11 a.m. and we haven't yet had breakfast. Alice has stabilised so Caroline bundles us out of the ward for some food.

'Go on, get some breakfast,' she says. She has stayed on long past the end of her shift. 'Nothing we can do for you if you faint in here. We only do babies.' She laughs.

Georgie and I sit in silence in the hospital café. We pick over the toast in front of us, eating because we know we have to, but deriving no joy from the process at all. Everything is on autopilot.

Georgie starts to sob and I reach my arm around her. The tiredness makes us vulnerable. My eyes sting as I start to reassure her that all will be well. Be strong for her, I tell myself.

'What happened to the baby next to Alice?' I ask, trying to change the subject. 'I noticed that the bay next door was empty. Has she been transferred?'

'She died in the night,' Georgie says.

So much for lightening the mood, I think, as an unfamiliar knot of fear grips my stomach.

'Oh, God. How?' I ask.

'I don't know,' Georgie replies. 'The poor parents.'

The reaper looming, ever present – his hands on our shoulders and his dank breath as he whispers his admonishments. His sharp accusations taunt me, he sneers at my arrogance and over-confidence. How dare you believe that all this would end well? How could you possibly think that after everything that's happened? What right do you have?

You don't make the rules here.

*

By lunchtime, Alice is steady, her oxygen requirements have reduced slightly and things are starting to look better. Grenville, the consultant in charge of the unit, has come to the ward now and is more sanguine about her chances.

That night we decide to stay close to the hospital and we spend the night at my parents' flat nearby.

The following morning, London's streets are dark as we make our way to the hospital.

We trudge through Horse Guards Parade, with its majesty and splendour; the sword-bearing Household Cavalry sentries a glorious anachronism in these modern times. Through the arches and right onto Whitehall, its tarmac shimmering beneath the Victorian streetlamps after this morning's much-needed downpour.

Statues in the morning mist: 'Good morning, Slim; morning, Alanbrooke; morning, Monty.'

There ahead of us the grand and ghostly Cenotaph, a reminder, as always, of the sacrifices made by our grandparents and great-grandparents.

SEPTEMBER

Passing Downing Street to our right, I wonder what affairs of great importance are being decided here right now, or is the Prime Minister just brushing his teeth and staring into space? It starts to rain again as we reach Parliament Square and the pinnacles of Big Ben's tower, the Houses of Parliament and Westminster Abbey reach high into the wet early-morning sky. My thoughts turn to the great men and women who have stood in their halls.

Left past Big Ben onto Westminster Bridge and there, for the first time ahead of us, stands St Thomas' Hospital, the ugly squat sixties block of white panels and windows, somewhat out of place in the company of the beautiful architecture surrounding it.

Unsightly though it is, this building holds greater significance than all of the others, symbolising our country's greatest hour, its greatest achievement: the Welfare State and the National Health Service. How lucky for our twins to have been born in this country, where a human being's wellbeing is held in such standing that health care is free for all, regardless of wealth, status or creed. The poverty of this building's appearance among the grandeur of those around it underlines the observation.

It's soon after 8 a.m. when we enter the hospital. Here come the night-shift nurses trudging through the hospital like an army of zombies, onwards inexorably to the train, to the bus and then to bed. A flashed smile and hello from one or two we recognise and I think of how much I admire them for the job they do.

Alice has had a steady night and is asleep still when we arrive, so we venture next door to Thomas's isolation ward. When we arrive at his incubator, standing alone in this large, empty room, there is a team of young doctors studying his charts and discussing the patient. The registrar asks us to follow him over to a corner of the room and starts to explain, 'We undertook a routine brain scan this morning.'

Oh, brain. Not good. The news we had most feared.

'The brain contains two reservoirs, which hold the cerebrospinal fluid. They are called ventricles. They have become very swollen and are getting to the stage where we are starting to get worried. There seem to be a few blood clots inside his brain and these are preventing the ventricles from draining – hence the swelling. This is quite a common affliction for young premmies – it's called hydrocephalus.'

'So what's the plan?' Georgie asks, now familiar with these conversations. We have become almost matter-of-fact about these issues now. The adrenalin rush of dread still hits us but we have learned to control it, to suppress it with the more pragmatic desire to understand how the doctors will solve this latest problem.

'Well,' he continues. 'We worry about this because the swelling prevents the brain from growing normally. The brain gets squashed against the inside of the skull by the swollen ventricles so it can't develop. The potential brain damage can be severe and long-lasting if the reservoirs are not drained.'

Our shoulders slump in unison.

'We are reassured by the fact that Thomas's condition remains stable, so there's no need to worry unnecessarily at this stage,' he says.

'We have had to undertake a short procedure though,' he explains. 'We need to extract some of the spinal fluid via a lumbar puncture to see whether the infection had caused meningitis.'

He pauses to make sure we're following, before continuing, 'Ordinarily, in order to perform this operation, we roll the patient into a ball to allow us to insert a needle into the column at the base of the spine. Unfortunately Thomas didn't respond well to this – his sats dropped quickly with the irritation of being bent double – so we now have to try a different tack.'

'Right . . . ?' I say expectantly.

'What we have to do is get to the spinal fluid through a different route,' he says.

'Right, OK, what route's that?' I ask.

'We stick a needle into his brain,' he replies, deadpan.

'What the fu—?' I exclaim.

The assembled medical staff look embarrassed by my reaction.

'Sorry, sorry,' I say. 'I meant to think that, but I didn't mean to say it.'

They smile, understanding, and the registrar continues.

'As you may know, newborns have a hole in their skulls which closes over as they grow. This is called the fontanelle. In this situation, it is a big advantage for us as we can easily pass a needle through the fontanelle and into the ventricles. We'll take a sample and send it away for testing. Obviously Thomas will be suitably managed so that he's settled throughout the procedure.'

I'm grateful for the fact that he's calling it a procedure. There's something reassuring about the word, suggesting as it does that this is a standard exercise and actually not HAVING A FUCKING BIG NEEDLE SHOVED INTO YOUR BRAIN WHEN YOU'RE ONLY A FEW WEEKS OLD, which, I have to admit, is rather the way I'm seeing it right now.

The moment only serves to highlight how ridiculously powerless we have become. The doctors could have told us that the best course of action was to throw Thomas out of the window and we would have to take their word for it.

He eventually says, 'We're going to need some space please to give us time to do the procedure, so can we ask you to give us an hour?'

I'm glad to be given the excuse not to have to witness this.

*

We wait downstairs in the restaurant while they undertake the operation. As the allotted time comes to a close, we make our way back through the hospital to the ward. My boots feel leaden as we walk. Always assume the worst news, because then you might be pleasantly surprised.

The reports are good. The procedure has been a success and several days later, tests confirm that there are no signs of infection in his spinal fluid. A week later the next brain scan shows that his ventricles have now reduced to an acceptable size so all is back to normal.

*

My outlet during this time, as has been the case through much of my life, is sport. Georgie understands well that without the ability to play sport, I will be insufferable. When we had started going out with each other at university, I had played football as often as four times a weekend, so she was very used to my not being around.

I play for two sides in London. One is a friendly side, Fenway Park, named, somewhat ambitiously, after the Boston Red Sox ground. It's a team of friends who have been playing together now for more than ten years. Our motto 'The swings are over there' (a remark once made by one of our centre halves to a particularly whingey opposition winger) nicely sums up the uncompromising manner with which we approach the game.

The other is a new team, FC London, a higher-quality outfit, playing in a West London League, where I'm tolerated rather than welcomed on account of my general lack of any kind of talent.

It's with this new team that I'm playing one September morning and becoming increasingly agitated by the fact that I'm having a stinker. There's no getting away from it and I see my teammates shoot glances at one another after yet another mistimed pass or missed header. The worse I get, the harder I try, but it doesn't seem to make any difference.

Half an hour into the game, their striker springs the offside trap and makes a beeline for the goal. I'm last man and immediately vexed by the fact that it's my fault that he's still onside, so I take off in pursuit. He stretches his legs and stretches his lead away from me, so I lunge despairingly at his disappearing heels.

My boot clips his heel and he tumbles like potatoes being emptied from a sack. He hits the floor and starts rolling and then writing in agony, clutching his shin.

I jump up, my blood boiling, I didn't even hit him there. What's he complaining about?

I stand and rush over to him, standing over him and shouting, 'What the fuck are you playing at? Trying to get me sent off. Get up, you pussy!'

My teammates are around me and pulling me off, but too

late. The opposition are piling in now and a twenty-man brawl has broken out: fists and slaps and handbags flailing and missing, occasionally connecting. The referee blasts his whistle repeatedly, but no one's listening. We're all standing there, in the middle of this twee West London park, a crowd of adults who should know better, swearing and swinging at one another. The dog walkers and Sunday morning joggers look on bemused. A father bundles his young family out of hearing range, away from the melee.

The fight gradually subsides and everyone steps back. The referee, somewhat inevitably, beckons me over and raises the red card.

'Early bath for you, big'un,' he says and I turn, trudging wearily towards the touchline.

My teammates watch me as I leave. I know what they're thinking. What's happened to the gentle giant? We've never seen him act like that.

As I stand alone under the shower in the changing room, I wonder at what I'm becoming. In twenty years of playing football, it's the first time I've ever been sent off in a match. Before the end of this season it will happen several more times as well.

12. October

The long, hot summer is finally coming to a close and the nights begin to draw in.

At home in Tooting we hold a nightly vigil in our bedroom to pray for safe passage for the twins through the coming night.

Georgie lights the candles on the dresser in our room and we stand side by side while she offers up a prayer. Something spiritual has been stirred by that miraculous night with Thomas. Maybe God is looking down on us. Maybe our prayers add 0.00001 per cent to the chance of their survival. Even if the chances are that slim, it's worth spending the moment to reflect on the day and give thanks for the fact that they are still with us.

And in early October, some of those prayers are answered as we are finally allowed to hold our babies for the first time, six weeks after their arrival. It's been a long wait, so this is a big day for us. Looking past the tubes, wires and the nurse squeezing the temporary ventilator bag over Alice's face, I can hardly believe that I am holding my daughter for the first time. For all the public show and cameras, it is an intensely private moment and I notice for the first time that Alice's eyes look similar to Georgie's in pictures I have seen of her as a toddler.

But still the twins' progress is being held up by their alarming tendency to drop their oxygen levels on a regular basis. The solution, we're told, is for a small duct between the heart and the lungs to be stapled closed. The duct is causing deoxygenated blood to flow to the body and is hampering forward progress. And so, we reluctantly agree for our babies to undergo this operation, we blithely sign consent forms, acknowledging that 'loss of life' is one potential outcome for such surgery, and we deliver our tiny babies to the vast, cold slab of the surgeon's table.

Outside we wait in the corridor and then in the waiting room. We sit and we wait: side by side on red, plastic, kids' chairs, no more than a foot high, with our knees pointing heavenwards from our seats. We look like circus clowns on tiny bikes. All the signs of nursery surround us – adding to the indignity. An uncomfortable and anxious hour passes before they come to get us.

Both operations pass smoothly and the babies are taken back to their ward.

*

By late October the scars from the twins' operations are healing nicely. The aim now is for the twins to come off their ventilators and onto an interim form of ventilation called 'continuous positive airways pressure' (CPAP), which provides a one-way flow of oxygen but allows the muscles around the lungs to do all the work.

Within a couple of weeks, this ambition is realised. Both twins make a significant breakthrough and come off their ventilators. These are very exciting moments, the first real sign of progress and the first tentative steps on the road to recovery and normality. Until now, all the good moments have been about them surviving infections, operations and disasters; for the first time they are now making progress of their own towards leaving hospital and surviving in the long term.

*

Both of our families have been a huge support during the events of the past few months and now my grandfather – my mother's father – has very generously offered to stand us a night out in a nearby hotel. He is keen for us to enjoy a night out and so, since things are steady, we gratefully, guiltily, take him up on his offer. The nurses bundle us out of the ward one Saturday afternoon, with reassuring words, telling us that they'll alert us if anything goes wrong.

We choose a hotel on the bounds of Hyde Park, a hotel which has a wonderful Roman-themed swimming pool on its top floor. As we lie by the pool, soaking up the last of the autumn's weakening sun, we can hear the hustle and bustle of the city's traffic down below. The moment seems to symbolise the bubble we have been living in for the past few months, while the rest of the world has been going about its business.

That evening we hit the booze and we hit it hard. Drinks in the room, drinks at the bar, drinks over dinner. We're keen to make up for lost time on the fun stakes. By the time our main course arrives, things have started to get a little hazy.

'Do you mind if we go back up to the room now?' Georgie says suddenly as we finish our main course.

'Sure,' I reply. I can't be certain, but I'm pretty sure she shaid that in a shuggeshtive way. It's been a long time since any sort of horizontal gymnastics were on the agenda. 'Let's go,' I say jumping up, anxious to hurry back to the room before the moment passes.

When we reach the room, it's evident that Georgie does have a role for me, but not the one I'd hoped for.

'Oh shit,' she says. 'I think I'm going to be sick.'

We rush into the bathroom, complete with double sink and gold taps, and Georgie slumps to her knees in front of the toilet.

'Can you hold my hair back, J?' she says as she retches and redecorates the inside of the undeniably fine toilet bowl.

'Sorry, J,' she mumbles between heaves. 'I've just realised that I haven't had a drink for a long, long time.' She throws up again.

It's true, first the IVF, then the pregnancy and more lately not drinking while she has been trying to provide breast milk for the babies. Perhaps we should have reintroduced alcohol more slowly . . .

Three months after their arrival, the twins are still fragile. But it turns out that our celebratory over-indulgence has not been without some justification. Confidence about their survival chances will have to wait, but we are about to enjoy the longest run of positive news yet.

13. Winter

The seasons are changing again and after the heat of summer, the warm cocoon of the neonatal intensive care unit now feels welcoming rather than oppressive.

There's welcome news from the twins too and the two-month period leading up to Christmas is a period of continual victories, as the twins gather themselves and climb the ladder to greater stability and long-term survival. Inch by inch they are crawling their way to health.

One by one we see the intravenous lines removed. First the paralysis drugs are taken away, then they are weaned off the palliatives like morphine and midazolam. One morning we arrive and Alice has no intravenous lines at all. And as she comes to real life – for the first time seeing the real world without the fog of drugs – she starts to battle even harder.

Slowly but surely the pressures are reduced on their ventilators and then the levels of oxygen are lowered until the doctors feel it is safe to put them onto CPAP.

One afternoon we arrive at Thomas's bed to find him surrounded by a team of doctors and nurses all studying his oxygen readings and watching him carefully. Unbelievably, amazingly his ventilator has been removed and he is now struggling to breathe on his own, without the in/out pressure of the ventilator to help him. We had hoped that this moment might be near, but had no idea that he had grown so much stronger in recent days to be capable of having the ventilator taken off. The assembled crowd grin at us as we enter.

Silky is the doctor in charge today. It's less than four months since she first spoke to us about their chances of survival, the night before their arrival, but it seems like a lifetime ago. She updates us on his progress.

'We've just this minute taken him off the ventilator.'

Our hearts leap at the news. What a milestone, what a breakthrough! It's obvious that not every member of the assembled throng of doctors and nurses needs to be there – they have all lived through Thomas's battles with him and now at this significant time, they want to be here to celebrate this moment with him too. Word has travelled fast around the unit and more nurses arrive to witness this leap forward.

'How's he coping on his own?' I ask.

'Well, he's finding it a bit of a struggle at the moment. As you can see, he's now on the lower level of breathing equipment, which feeds oxygen to him via a tube in his nose. But,' she tells us, 'much of the oxygen is being lost through his open mouth. His sats don't seem to be picking up though so we may need to reintroduce him to full ventilation unless we have a solution.'

'What do you suggest?' asks Georgie.

'Well, we tried a dummy in this situation once before. It

should have the effect of closing his mouth and retaining more of the oxygen from the pipe. Are you happy for us to try that?'

I look at Georgie, remembering the conversation prior to their births where we agreed that we didn't want the children to use dummies. How our priorities have changed.

A dummy is found and in it goes. Thomas's sats leap to normal levels and it's obvious he's happy with the new solution.

It's a small thing, but it underlines how far the goalposts have shifted since before the twins arrived. The shift in priorities from the way we used to talk about them while they were still *in utero* has been significant. All the rules and expectations have been flung out. Getting the twins through this experience to the other side is all that matters – whatever it takes.

*

Later we wander down the hospital's long corridor, Georgie and I, musing about and discussing the progress we are finally seeing. As we walk, the corridor is briefly lit by the bright colours of day bursting through the plate-glass window. We stop and turn as one. There, beyond the hospital wall, stands the Palace of Westminster, glorious in the morning sun.

We step out into the day. The Palace is lit bright yellow in splendid contrast to the azure of the wintry morning sky behind it. Only our hot breath clouds the view of Big Ben's tower, standing tall and all-seeing, the golden ornamentation at its peak glistening in the sun.

Our hearts are lifted and we stand, admiring the view for a few brief minutes. For me the sight seems designed just for us, to remind us of just how far we've come and to remain strong for the battles ahead. We're still a few weeks away from the twins' due date and yet so much has happened in their short lives already. I can't help thinking that even now, they should still be tucked up inside their mother.

We breathe in the cold, fresh air and consider how far we have come already. Eventually, we turn back for the hospital.

*

In the following days, the twins start to spend short bursts of time off the CPAP and they are moved to nasal cannulas. These devices provide a low steady flow of oxygen through a small pipe attached to the nostrils.

One bright winter's day, Ernie is looking after Alice again and she is smiling as we arrive.

'How would you two like to give Alice a bath today?' she asks.

We have longed for this privilege for each of the eighty-four days that the twins have been here.

She talks us through the protocol, instructing us how to hold Alice, how to keep her tiny fragile frame from slipping under the water and how best to bathe her with all the inconvenience of her wires and attachments.

Georgie is beaming as she holds Alice in the water, gently splashing the water up onto her body. Alice seems perplexed by this unusual experience but she doesn't protest and holds Georgie's eyes in her gaze. The trusting bond between them is fully evident for the first time.

The weeks pass and as the twins progress we become increasingly confident that they are putting the dramas of those early months behind them. We long to see them together. Despite the recent progress, they are still being kept apart due to Thomas's ongoing infection. He has been in isolation for nearly three months now and the twins haven't yet shared the same cot or touched each other since they were in the womb. We yearn for the day when they will be reunited.

And so, on Christmas Eve, the nurses on the ward give us an early Christmas present.

We are sitting alongside Thomas's cot, readying him for the following day's celebrations. Georgie has bought a stocking to attach to the end of his cot and is busy tying it on.

We look up as the ward doors open and silently, surreptitiously, nurse Caroline enters Thomas's room, wheeling his twin sister in her cot.

She holds her finger to her lips. This has clearly not been sanctioned by the powers that be, but our hearts leap that the twins are about to be reunited for the first time since they had been separated at their birth.

'Happy Christmas!' she chimes. 'We thought it was high time that Alice met her brother again.'

Georgie is beaming. 'Oh, thank you. What a lovely surprise,' she says.

'Go on then.' Caroline says. 'Pop her in.'

Georgie gently lifts Alice out of her cot and lays her down with her brother. The twins take one look at each other and burst into tears.

Perhaps they've got so used to feeling like they were the only one getting all the attention that they're disappointed to realise that they are going to have to share.

But they soon settle down and it's wonderful to see them lying alongside each other, suspiciously eyeing one another.

Caroline says, 'We know the doctors have been keeping

them apart because of the risk of Thomas's infection, but they're being overly cautious. We figured you guys have been through enough and that you might enjoy a little Christmas present.'

We've all been through a lot. Thomas and Alice. Georgie and me. But it's obvious that these amazing nurses and doctors have been wounded by the twins' experiences as well. They have invested so much time, effort and love in seeing our children to health. This tiny victory is for them as well as us.

*

I continue with my unusual commute to work. I drive in to see the twins early in the morning, spend an hour or two at the hospital with them before work. Some work days start at 7 a.m. for me, so the nurses become used to seeing me arriving at 5 a.m., when they provide me with a report on the night. Then in the evenings I return to spend another hour or two with them and then to take Georgie home. She herself rises early and catches the train in to the hospital where she spends the whole day with the twins. The ward has become her pattern, her life.

One wet morning, early in December, I'm driving to work. I have Test Match Special playing on the radio. The England cricket team are playing a test match in Galle, in Sri Lanka. The Sri Lankan commentator is describing the idyllic scene.

'It is a beautiful, warm day here in Galle,' he begins, a wonderful lilt to his voice, all rolled R's and exaggerated pronunciation. 'From our position in the commentary box, we have a beautiful view of the cricket ground and behind it the wonderful fortress, which overlooks the pitch here. The flags are fluttering on the ramparts and it's a clear day out to sea.'

I've never been to Galle, but I'm momentarily transported away from the miserable rain and the thudding of my windscreen wipers to the tranquil image he describes.

'Good morning to you if you are just waking up in England,' he continues. 'Perhaps you are reclining in your favourite easy chair, with a mug of your favourite Earl Grey and a copy of the London *Times*?'

'Haha!' I laugh, relishing this outdated image of a time when Britain ruled the waves. 'No!' I shout at the radio, 'I'm driving to the fucking hospital at 5 a.m. in the lashing rain!'

*

Georgie is settling into her routine now with greater confidence and I can tell that she is even starting to enjoy her role as a mother. For many months, the agony of the question of their survival had prevented either of us from getting any enjoyment out of the experience of being new parents, but now that they are getting stronger, Georgie's shoulders have come down and she is relaxing into the job of being Mum.

It's not the way she would have wanted, an endless stream of nurses taking the lead in caring for her twins when she would much rather have that responsibility herself. But as the weeks pass, she steps into that role until eventually it is her instructing the nurses what to do, rather than the other way around.

One weekend morning we arrive in the hospital car park and are drawing up to a space, when a car barges through and steals the spot. I wind down the window to remonstrate with the driver.

A young man jumps out of the car with a look of terror behind his eyes.

I start to shout at him when he says, 'Sorry, my daughter's not well, she's been here seven days and I need to see her.'

Seven days, I think to myself, try four months! But I see the look in his eyes and remember how it felt at the beginning – the panic, dread and unfamiliarity of it all. It occurs to me that hospital life has become second nature to us now. We are part of the furniture, we have been here longer than many of the staff caring for our kids and seeing this young man's face reminds me how far we've come. Several medical staff have recently asked us if we are doctors because of the terminology we use. If we're not careful we'll become institutionalised!

We arrive on the ward to find Alice has chocolate stains around her mouth and on her pillow.

'Who's been feeding Alice chocolate?' Georgie calls to the assembled nurses.

They shuffle sheepishly from one foot to another.

'Er,' says one.

'It's eight o'clock in the morning!' says Georgie exasperated and trying not to laugh.

I start laughing, amused by the scene and pleased to see Georgie at last able to take the lead role in caring for the twins. For months parenting has been happening to us. Now it's beginning to be done by us, which is just as it should be.

*

Between Christmas and New Year, both twins are finally deemed healthy enough to be admitted to the special care baby unit. After our months in Intensive Care, we had longed for the day when we would arrive at the neonatal unit and turn left into SCBU rather than right into NICU, the home for the really sick babies.

On New Year's Eve, we bring in the New Year in style with our little ones. The SCBU at St Thomas' is on the sixth floor, occupying the corner of the hospital directly opposite the Houses of Parliament. It's an ideal vantage point for London's New Year firework display. We, along with a small group of parents and medical staff, watch as the country's biggest firework display kicks off no more than 200 yards away from us.

The inky night sky glows with the bright colours and the boom of the explosions sends reverberations through the windows that we are standing at. Georgie is next to me and I reach my arm around her shoulder. Her face is lit with the red, yellow and blue of the fireworks and we smile at one another.

'Here's to more luck in the New Year,' I say.

'. . . and bringing our babies home,' she whispers as she reaches up to kiss me.

As tens of thousands of pounds of fireworks are exploded on the Thames close before our eyes, it seems that the Mayor of London is sending his own special note of congratulation to the four of us.

Over the coming months, the babies continue to make great progress and by now we are being drilled in the ways of managing with the twins once we get them home. Finally, after months of day-by-day survival, we feel brave enough to ask the question, 'Are they going to make it now?' Only now are we relatively sure that the answer will be the one that we want to hear. So we ask Anthony Kaiser, one of the consultants on the ward, who has been attending to the twins since they came to SCBU.

'Oh yes,' says Anthony with a surprised look, when we put the question to him. 'They're out of the woods now.' It's clear he has been convinced for weeks now of the fact they will survive, but we have just been too afraid to believe it and too superstitious to ask.

After the months of hoping and praying for the moment, it looks like we are going to get our babies home.

*

It's a cold February evening and I leave work at 6 p.m. to spend my evening with the twins. I reach the special care unit at 6.30 in time for Alice's bath and bottle. She is starting to spend a little time during the day without the nasal cannula – breathing entirely on her own. It's lovely to see her face and increasingly chubby cheeks free from attachments for the first time. The bath is ready and I have finished undressing her so I lift her into my arms. Looking down I notice her chubby bum has acquired the mottled orange-peel effect hated by women the world over and I feel so proud that my little girl has got enough meat on her to get cellulite.

And then it strikes me. I'm holding Alice, just Alice, nothing else. No wires, no IV lines, no breathing apparatus, no clothes. Just my beautiful, pink, soft baby. Alice. I can whirl her round my head and do as many pirouettes as I want to. Not that I want to, you understand, it's just that for the first time, nothing's going to get tangled. It's a special moment.

Finally free from the connections that have sustained her life to this point, Alice is living entirely under her own steam.

*

Early one Saturday morning we are at home preparing to leave for the hospital when the phone rings. It is Linda, a nurse on the ward.

'Sorry to disturb you both,' she apologises. Her usually cheerful voice is serious. 'It's Alice. I'm so sorry, she's back in intensive care. She's gone backwards overnight and is on a lot of oxygen again. We wanted you to know. You might want to come in.'

'OK, thanks for letting us know, Linda. We're on our way.'

Oh God, not again.

We rush to the hospital. Alice has once again been walloped with the paralysing agent and is lifeless, save for the ventilator forcing air into her lungs. Her saturations are running low. The sight of her with the ventilator tube and IV lines in her again is too much.

'Just popping to the loo,' I say to Georgie. She looks up at me quizzically.

I lock myself in the cubicle, bang down the toilet seat, slump with my head in my hands and start to sob.

I have come to love my little girl in a way that I hadn't at the start of her life. I spent so much of those early weeks thinking that they were going to die that I forced myself to be detached from loving the twins. My primary concern has been to catch Georgie when the inevitable happened, but as each day passed and they survived, I slowly started to believe that they would make it and to love them as a proper father should. To have come all that way and dared to hope . . . it is terrifying to be so close to losing Alice again.

I wonder uselessly whether I will ever be able to find hope again.

*

By the time I return to the ward the doctors and nurses are upbeat and sanguine about Alice's prospects.

One of them explains, 'This happens to premmies every now and again and they tend to fight back quickly. Especially when they are as strong as Alice has become. We don't want you to worry too much.'

Needless to say they are right, and soon they withdraw the paralysing drug to allow her to wake and breathe on her own.

One of the nurses, Darcy, explains that this in itself presents a problem. 'As she wakes up, she will feel the ventilation tube in her throat and be unhappy about the feeling in her throat. The secret is to keep her calm while she comes around until she is strong enough to breathe on her own, but it's going to take a number of hours.'

Darcy has grown very attached to Alice during the previous months. His gruff, Kiwi exterior belies a heart of gold and a determination to see the best possible outcome for Alice. He knows this is going to be a difficult day for her and whoever looks after her, but despite this he has volunteered for the role. He stands with her throughout the day, stroking her head and talking to her, keeping her cool and reassured, and monitoring her statistics for signs of deterioration. He forgoes his lunch break and stands with her for the full twelve hours of his shift.

By the evening, Darcy has nursed Alice back to strength and she is returned to SCBU.

Once again I am deeply humbled by the strength, love and skill of these new friends.

14. April

'It's time for Alice to go home.'

Anthony Kaiser is smiling as he delivers these words to us. The assembled nurses are also smiling. It's clear that they should be working elsewhere on the unit, but they have chosen to be here when the news is delivered to us to share the picture on our faces when we receive this news.

'Thomas won't be far behind his sister,' he continues, 'but while he's having these breath-holding episodes, we want to keep him in for a few weeks longer.' Thomas has been keeping us all on our toes recently. At the slightest irritation he has been holding his breath. As his colour changes from pink to a bright purple our anxiety rises – these episodes seem to last an eternity – but eventually he relents with a huge, life-giving gulp of air.

But his sister has done it and Georgie and I are thrilled. It's the words we have waited nine months to hear. She has overcome the odds to achieve this wonderful victory, for her, for her brother and for her parents.

'Life's going to be busy for you when the twins come home, so I'm going to advise that you take some time to escape for a few days,' Anthony goes on. 'It's your last chance!'

A week later, we follow Anthony's advice and head down to Cornwall for a break. It says a lot about how far the twins have come that we feel confident enough to leave them. We drive down one Friday night and stay in a tiny hotel called the Lugger, a seventeenth-century inn in a tiny fishing village called Portloe on the Roseland Peninsula. The setting is picture-postcard perfect; the village surrounded by hills and cliffs on three sides, the sea on the other. The hotel sits down by the water at the bottom of the steep hill that leads down through the village.

The day after our arrival we walk along the coastal path to nearby Caerhays Castle, where we spend several hours walking around the Castle's gardens and enjoying a relaxing lunch. It's drizzling when we leave the castle to return to Portloe, and the sea mist closes in on the coast path, reducing visibility to little more than a few metres. The going is precarious and occasionally we stumble as we pick our way along the cliff top. Sometimes I lead, sometimes it's Georgie. We talk to one another as we go, about the traumas and miracles that we have witnessed, and sometimes guiding one another with warnings about the path underfoot.

But as we trudge through the mist, the sun eventually starts to make its presence felt and it peeks through the cloud. The fog lifts and as we turn the final corner around the headland into Portloe, it suddenly becomes a beautiful spring afternoon.

The sun sparkles on the water, which laps against the craggy cliffs of this beautiful corner of England.

So we sit down together on the grassy bank up above the village and drink in the view. Below we can hear the distant noise of the village going about its business. The gentle wind clanks the rigging of the small handful of vessels that have been brought up onto the sand.

'It's going to be a big test for us,' says Georgie.

'Yes,' I agree.

The sun feels warm on our faces and we lie back on the grass.

'How are you feeling about it?' I ask.

'Excitement and trepidation,' she replies.

'Same,' I say.

'I'm looking forward to being a mother,' she says. 'I haven't had that opportunity for the past nine months. I can't thank the nurses enough for what they've done for us, but it's been hard standing by and letting them do the job that I was supposed to do all this time.'

It's true. This passage of our lives has been undeniably tough, but we haven't really yet experienced real parenthood. Soon the four of us will be on our own and in many ways, that's when we'll find out what we're made of as parents.

There's a gentle breeze coming up the hill now, cooling my face and counteracting the warmth of the sun. My head feels fuzzy and I start to dose.

*

It's much later when I wake and the sun is starting its descent behind the opposite hill. It feels colder already. Georgie is awake.

TWO FOR JOY

'Ready?' she says.
'Ready,' I reply.

15. Home

Two weeks later, I find myself at the sixth-floor window in NICU once again, staring out into the hospital's garden below.

I remind myself of the day back in September when I had stood here and wondered what colour the grass would be when the twins finally came home. Back then we'd been told December and here we are another four months later than that, with Alice the first to be released after 259 days. The grass has seen all four seasons since we first came here. In a few months' time it will start to brown with summer again.

At last it's time to take Alice home and we strap her into the double buggy that we have bought for the twins. To her left, on the side where her brother should be – will be in a few weeks – we have stuffed a collection of all of the gifts and clobber that she has acquired during the first nine months of her life – teddies, blankets, posters made by the nurses.

We say our farewells to the nurses and wheel Alice out of the neonatal ward forever. As Georgie and I stand in the lift lobby with Alice in her buggy, Georgie squeezes my hand three times. We've done it.

The lift arrives and the three of us climb in.

A new father rushes up to the lift and holds the door. His partner wheels their newborn baby daughter into the lift.

As the lift descends to the ground floor, he looks into Alice's buggy, smiles and says, 'Congratulations!'

'Thanks' I reply. 'You too.'

I wonder how long they have been here. Three days? A week?

For Alice, it's been nine months.

Congratulations indeed.

*

We drive home and pause on the threshold of our new home with our new family member. I photograph Georgie standing with Alice in her arms in the doorway of our home. Georgie looks exhausted, and no wonder.

We walk through to the living room and Alice's eyes stand on stalks to see the bookshelves in our living room, the pictures on the wall and the fire glowing. She's never seen anything like this – anything so normal – in her short life.

It reminds me of a moment several months back, when I saw a full-term baby newly born and brought down to the unit for an overnight stay. Not an hour old, the look of wonderment on this baby's face was something special to behold as he gazed around the room. But it only served to remind me of what we had missed out on with our own babies. To see Alice now as she is introduced to her new environment, to her home, I feel glad that I am experiencing her amazement at the world now.

It feels as if she is seeing things as they should be for the first time.

*

Several weeks later and Thomas follows his sister home.

We have asked if we can hold a going-home party on the unit to say thank you to the medical staff who have saved our babies' lives.

We stand in the inappropriate surroundings of the breast-feeding room, sipping champagne from plastic cups and eating celebratory cakes off paper plates. Looking round the crowded room, I feel an enormous surge of affection for these amazing people, strangers just nine months earlier but now cemented in our lives and memories forever.

Here in one corner is Dr Bal, whom both grannies have taken a shine to and who told us to hang on to seemingly futile hope in those early days. And Ernie, who looked after Thomas on the first day and who cried when she visited him months later in SCBU because she couldn't believe that he had made it. Darcy, who dedicated so much time to caring for Alice in particular and brought her back from the brink when she collapsed again so recently.

Then there is the wonderful, one-in-a-million Caroline, whom we have asked to be godmother to the twins, who gave us hope one morning in January by telling us that she had had a dream that she was playing on the swings with the twins at some distant time in the future. I wonder as I look at her whether this vision will one day become a reality.

Laura and Louisa, who bought all sorts of gifts for the twins – Louisa who was unable to resist spending all her hard-earned cash on internet shopping while she was looking after Thomas on night shifts and Laura who would update us as to Alice's positive or negative night by simply saying 'she's been a princess' or 'she's been a pudding' in her Welsh lilt.

Shelley and Mel, the double act who were always on duty when the twins retrenched and who saved Alice's life on the first night by refusing to believe that she was gone.

And Dr Tim. Always honest, even when it was the last thing he wanted to be. Amazingly he has tears in his eyes. He can't believe that the twins are both going home. Perhaps none of them can believe it?

How to thank these amazing miracle workers who have poured so much effort, skill and love into saving our babies and nurturing them to health? To have come to know these people and to have grown close to them . . . I suddenly realise how my life has been enriched by the experience of these past nine months.

It has been a privilege to be surrounded by so many wonderful people, pulling together with all their skills, their faith and their love for the single purpose of saving children. Our children.

Our thank-you letter says something of the way we feel:

> Where do we start with a thank-you to a group of people who collectively have saved our babies' lives and then nursed them to health? How do we convey the profound feeling of gratitude for all the skill with which our babies have been rescued from several

near-death experiences and handed back to us today looking as regal and unconcerned as if they'd just woken from a short snooze? Needless to say, these questions have been at the front of our minds for many months now and we're still no closer to figuring out the answer! Somehow the words 'thank you' just come up a bit short.

But here it is anyway, 'thank you'. Thank you for getting Thomas and Alice out of the starting blocks and for giving them a chance at life. Thank you for giving us a glimmer of hope when all hope seemed to have gone. Thank you for bringing light into some very dark moments. Thank you for always knowing what to say and for having the courage to say it. Thank you for never trying to make it sound better than it was. Thank you for helping us to stay positive throughout. Thank you for the hugs and the shoulders to cry on. Thank you for all the laughs and fun we've had. Thanks for treating us as your friends and welcoming us into your world. Thank you for the love and dedication you gave to our twins. And thank you for enabling us to realise the gift of parenthood.

16. Springtime

At last we realise our dream of walking our babies through the park in their buggy. The twins draw admiring smiles and coos from the people that walk past.

An old lady stops to peer into the buggy.

She says, 'Twins, how wonderful. You really are blessed'.

Georgie and I give knowing looks to one another, looks that acknowledge our secret, the secret that says all that glitters is not gold.

Then I say, 'Blessed? Yes, we bloody well are . . .'

And every night I go in to Thomas and Alice's room, I put my ear up close against their faces and listen to the quiet but significant whisper of their breathing and I wonder at the miracles we have witnessed.

PART 2

A LIFE LESS
ORDINARY

17. Father Figure

Now that we are home, we are slowly but surely feeling our way in to the daily routine of being new parents.

Last summer, before the twins arrived, we had just exchanged contracts on a new house in Streatham in South London. With the twins' early arrival and questions about the likelihood of their survival, there had been a sudden uncertainty about whether we would actually need a bigger house and our plans to buy were delayed. Luckily, the sellers were patient and a few months into the twins' lives we decided to be bold and to go ahead and buy the new house. It is a terraced, brick, semi-detached house, near Streatham Common. The rooms are large and the ceilings tall and we suddenly feel like kids playing at being grown-ups in this big house with our small family. Given the gamble we took in buying it, this house has come to symbolise the twins' survival.

TWO FOR JOY

We have had nine months to get ready for their homecoming so their bedroom is a special space. Georgie has hung old-fashioned Beatrix Potter frames from her own bedroom when she was a child. The two cots sit alongside each other with a narrow chest of drawers in between. A stranger would have no difficulty identifying which bed belongs to which baby; Alice's bed is bedecked in pink, from the teddies to the duvet cover, and Thomas's likewise in blue. There are so many teddies there's barely room for the twins themselves in their cots – a legacy of their long stay in hospital and the endless stream of visitors and well-wishers. Even the wooden cots themselves are a symbol of the twins' victory; they are the twins' first real beds after the impersonal incubators and warming trays of the hospital.

It's a tall room and my mother's home-made yellow, gingham curtains hang in the high window in the far corner.

Soon we are into the normal routine that we have hoped for and spent many months praying for. But it's not long before I am longing for the security and additional support of the hospital. How ungrateful! I think to myself, but I can't hide from the fact that I'm finding it hard.

Feeding the twins typically takes a couple of hours because they are both suffering badly with reflux, Thomas in particular. Given their low size and weight, we are encouraged to feed them five times a day, so all in all, ten hours a day are spent feeding the twins, preparing food, washing up and clearing up sick. Every mealtime is a source of creeping frustration as meals are force fed and come back up in equal-sized doses.

There is very little time for anything else during the day.

But into the cracks in the schedule we cram visits from physiotherapists, health visitors, occupational therapists, social workers . . . The days are filled with nothing but caring for the twins and life becomes very one-dimensional.

The days are full of repetition and, if I'm honest, drudgery. I long for the opportunity to do other things, anything that represents a change from the tight timetable of feeding and physiotherapy. In most households there's an argument about who does the washing up – it's seen as a chore that no one wants to do. For me, it's something of a treat to be allowed to stand for five minutes with my hands in hot soapy water, staring absently out of the kitchen window.

Nor does the work end at night time. The impact of all of those collapsed lungs and months spent on ventilators means that the twins' lungs will never be perfect. So, at the foot of their beds, oxygen machines hum, carrying still crucial oxygen up to the twins through plastic pipes. Georgie and I lie in bed at night, listening to the huffing of the machine as it sends another burst of life-giving oxygen along its pipe.

Fscht (in), *pffffft* (out).

Sats monitors connect to their toes, bleeping their warnings when the twins' oxygen levels fall below a certain point. We jump up and out of bed every time the alarm sounds, to check them, reposition them, increase their oxygen; do whatever it takes to get their oxygen back up to a safe level.

I can't help wondering about the future as I lie in bed at night.

I'm so proud of how the children have got through the horrors of their early arrivals and survived. But I can't help thinking that this might be the happiest time for us – the only time when everything feels really normal.

What if they are disabled? Will we be able to cope?

*

One Sunday morning, several weeks after the children have come home, I decide to get the twins out of bed and down to breakfast on my own. At six o'clock in the morning, I hear them starting to stir.

'You stay there,' I say to Georgie, kissing the small, unkempt crown of hair poking out from the top of the duvet. With any luck she'll stay put for a little while longer and I can manage the twins' breakfast myself.

I rise, dress quickly and go into the twins' bedroom. I lift the twins from their beds, change them, dress them and prepare to take them down to breakfast. I carry Thomas downstairs to the kitchen first. Over in the corner of the small kitchen at the back of our house we have a soft area for the twins to lie on but all the cushions are still packed away.

Damn, I think to myself, there's nowhere to put him down.

'Always get everything ready in the kitchen before you bring the twins in here.' Georgie's voice in my head.

Over in the far corner, there is a hard chair with a big cushion on it. 'There we go,' I whisper and I lay Thomas gently on his back on the soft green cushion. I turn to gather up the pile of cushions and rugs and start to lay them out into a nest on the kitchen floor for Thomas.

As I turn back to pick him up, the world suddenly goes into slow motion. Before it happens, I can already see what the outcome is going to be.

Thomas is arching his back on the chair and has moved right to the edge and now, with one final push, he flips himself backwards off the chair, head first and down onto the hard slate floor of the kitchen.

There is a sickening thud as his head hits the floor.

'Oh shit.'

The world stops. Thomas is still on the floor as I cross the room.

'Shit, oh shit.'

I reach Thomas and gather him up. He is holding his breath and turning a nasty shade of grey.

'J?' Georgie has heard the bang and is calling from upstairs.

Under my breath, 'Oh fuck, oh fuck, oh fuck.'

'J?!'

'Oh no, please. Shit!'

Thomas projectile vomits across the kitchen and across me.

'Oh shit. No, no, no! Thomas!' I hold him in front of me, my arms outstretched, desperately searching for signs that he is OK.

Georgie appears bleary-eyed, hair askew, still wrapping her dressing gown around her. 'What's going on?'

"Er, I, er, I put him, um, on the chair for a bit and he . . .'

'*What?*' she shouts.

Suddenly the bit about putting him on the chair didn't sound so super intelligent.

'What have I said about getting everything ready first?!' she says.

'Oh fuck,' I say. 'Oh no, oh God please.' After everything he's been through, how could I have been so stupid!

I'm shaking, holding my son close, both of us covered in sick and Thomas now screaming the house down.

Georgie reaches for the phone and calls our friends in the neonatal unit back at St Thomas'.

'Bring him in to A & E,' they say. 'It's probably nothing, but because he's been sick after a bang to the head, we should take every precaution. We'll tell them to expect you.'

This doesn't make me feel a great deal better. The four of us rush to the car as quickly as we can.

'Do you think he's going to be OK?' I ask desperately in the car.

'I just don't know, J,' Georgie replies angrily. We sit in silence the rest of the way to A & E. Thoughts of the worst kind occupy my mind.

After everything that has gone before, how could I have been so reckless and so stupid? What does this mean? Thomas is already at an extremely high risk of suffering from brain damage, what is this going to mean to his prospects?

I feel physically sick as we reach the hospital. It is a sensation I haven't felt for several months; the sensation of not feeling like eating or even being able to eat.

A nurse and young doctor arrive and run through the routine of checking Thomas over.

'He's fine,' the doctor confirms and I start to relax again. 'Just a bit of a bang. There won't be any significant side effects.'

The relief seems to spill out of my pores. Is it obvious to people? Is it obvious to Georgie? Clearly Sunday mornings are going to be decidedly 'lie-in-lite' for Georgie over the coming weeks.

'Shall we drop in to the neonatal unit to see our friends while we're here?' I ask, my positive mood returning. I'm also keen to thank them for their advice this morning.

'Yes, let's say a quick hello,' says Georgie. I'm grateful she's so forgiving.

As we arrive in these familiar surroundings we are greeted by Darcy.

Darcy is beaming, delighting in my discomfort at this embarrassing episode. We've got to know each other well over the past few months.

He smiles as he says, 'For fuck's sake, James, we spend nine months saving his life and the second you get him home, you're chucking him on his head!'

We all laugh. I feel like a prize tit, but once again I'm relieved that these wonderful people have ways and means of making us feel better about life, even when I can't imagine that I can do any worse.

*

Some months after the twins come home, I find myself home alone one evening, collapsed on the sofa in our sitting room, absent-mindedly flicking through the channels.

I come across a medical drama on television. The set and situation look familiar . . .

. . . An expectant father is sitting in the quiet room of a hospital delivery ward. A doctor comes into the room wearing a pained expression that looks horribly familiar to me.

The doctor speaks. 'I'm afraid that there have been complications with the delivery.'

He sits down next to the father whose face turns ashen. His eyes are expectant – what's coming next?

Slowly, the doctor starts to speak, 'I'm afraid that your son did not survive the trauma of the birth. I'm so sorry; he passed away several minutes ago.'

The father's face wears a horribly familiar expression. 'Can I see my wife?' he asks.

The doctor's face turns white. 'I'm so sorry,' he says. 'She has sustained very significant brain damage during the delivery. I'm sorry but I think it is highly unlikely that she will ever regain consciousness.'

The father sits, slumped and slack-jawed, uncomprehending.

A nurse in scrubs enters the room clutching the tiny body of the man's son, swaddled like any normal baby in its blankets.

'Would you like to hold your son?' she offers. She hands the baby to him. . . .

The memory of the third night with Thomas comes flooding back to me and hits me like a steam train. We had come so close to having to hold our dying son as he gave his last, pathetic breath and now I am seeing that imagined moment being played out here.

I start crying. Uncontrollably.

I've often read about, but never before experienced, the sensation of uncontrolled crying but now I know what they mean.

I cry and I cry and I cry and there's nothing I can do to stop it.

*

I have always led a charmed life. Good luck has followed me and everything has generally come up smelling of roses. A colleague at work has even sarcastically christened me Golden Balls. It now seems that things are going in a very different direction.

I arrive at my desk at work one morning after the short commute to work.

My phone rings – it's Georgie.

'J, can you come home please?' she says.

'What's happened?' I ask.

'The ceiling's fallen in in the twins' bedroom,' she replies.

'What!' I say. 'Were they in there? Are they OK?'

'Yes, they're fine. It happened just now when I was getting them up, we were all in there.' I can tell from her trembling voice that she has been shaken by what has just happened. 'A huge lump of ceiling has fallen down between their cots. Thomas was on my knee in the corner, but Alice was in her cot and she's been hit. She's fine, but it looks like a building site.'

'Shit,' I say. 'I'm on my way.'

When I get home, the twins' room reminds me of the TV footage of the Brighton bombing. It is covered in rubble, plaster and dust. A large piece of ceiling is still held in place by the wallpaper above and hangs down like an angry wound. The room is covered in dust and between the twins' cots a large lump of concrete has dropped on top of the bedside drawers, smashing the top surface.

Georgie joins me, 'I dread to think what might have happened if that lump had fallen a foot either side, while the twins were still in their cots,' she says.

'If it wasn't for bad luck, as the old song goes, we wouldn't have no luck at all,' I reply.

'Better get a dustpan and brush,' she says, laughing.

'Screw that,' I reply. 'We're going to need a JCB and a skip.'

And before I know it, we're both laughing at the absurdity of it all.

*

We decide to get away for a few days to recharge our batteries. Mum and Dad have friends with a house in Frinton-on-Sea on the Essex coast and they kindly agree to let us take their house for a week. Frinton is where we used to come for day trips when I was growing up in Suffolk. It is a reminder of a bygone era and, like many English seaside towns, it is populated by octogenarians. 'Harwich for the Continent, Frinton for the incontinent,' as Dad is fond of joking.

It is our first time away as a family and as we pack the car, we begin to realise what a major operation this short break is going to be. The four of us haven't been away together before. In addition to all of the clobber you might expect as a new family – bedding, clothing, buggy, toys – we also have to find room in the car for oxygen machines, back-up oxygen cylinders, sats monitors, medicines, syringes.

'How long are we going away for?' asks Georgie with a smile as we survey our new estate car brimful with baby stuff and equipment. It is like a cross between a delivery van and an ambulance.

'To the Essex Riviera.' I laugh. 'And quick about it.'

We share a wonderful week by the sea, living the dream that we had held so close during the dark days and nights in the neonatal unit. The dream is one of a normal family, going about their holiday business – moseying along the promenade with our dog, building sandcastles on the beach, taking in the shops and enjoying coos of admiration from passers-by at our beautiful twins. It feels normal and for the first time it feels wonderful.

The house even has a swimming pool and one day we wake

to warm autumn sunshine and so we decide to take a dip. We pull the twins' swimming costumes on for the first time, excited about the new experience we are all about to enjoy together. The twins' faces have apprehension writ large across them as we step down into the pool but as we enter the water for the first time, they break out into winning smiles.

Georgie is lifting Alice up and down, splashing her against the water and they are both giggling.

I lean back and start to move backwards through the water with Thomas on my chest. I hold his legs out in front and encourage him to splash the water with his feet. He is squeaking his delight at the new sensation and his body starts to tremble with the excitement. Suddenly his head tilts back and his body extends ramrod straight in front of me. I have to grip him tightly to keep from dropping him.

'Woah,' I say, struggling to hold him above the water. He relaxes and I say to Georgie, 'Has he done that before?'

'Yes,' she replies. 'It tends to be when he's excited or uncomfortable. The physio said the arching is something to keep an eye on. Alice too.'

I don't ask her to explain because Thomas is now giggling like crazy, loving every second of the experience of being waterborne, and it's a magical moment, not one to be disrupted by worries about the future.

Later we walk with the twins down to the sea front, along the promenade and then back up the slope to the greensward above the water. We park the buggy up alongside a bench on the grassy hill and take a seat. Lolly curls up at our feet, Georgie burrows under my arm and we sit in silence, cocooned against the breeze coming off the North Sea. Away to our right, we can see the golf club beyond the long sloping curve of the greensward; down below us the seemingly never-ending row of brightly coloured beach huts bringing to me happy memories of holidays past; and, straight ahead, the boundless sight of the sea, shimmering beneath the sun, its glare reflecting in a mottled path across the water.

Georgie sighs happily.

'Winning?' I ask.

'Yep,' she replies. 'Always.'

18. The Song Remains the Same

Fscht, pfffft.

At night, the twins' ventilators continue to hum quietly in their room, pushing their life-giving breaths into the twins' still-tiny bodies.

Fscht, pfffft.

The symphony to our life.

They are a constant reminder of the twins' fragile state but we are now sufficiently confident to have removed the oxygen saturation probes from their toes at night. So the occasional *bing-bing* of the monitors' alarms, which had us sitting up bolt upright in bed, has stopped. Instead, without the safety net of the monitors, we lie awake, wondering whether the twins are still breathing! Every now and then, one of us will get out of bed – a cough, a choke, or even nothing at all will prompt us to go and check. Just to be sure. Be better off with the bloody probes on, frankly.

Despite these steps forward, we are no closer to learning the twins' fate, even though they are now more than a year old. It is still unclear to us what sort of future lies ahead for them.

Georgie and I are settling into the routine of our new life. The traumatic memories of the twins' early months still surprise us from time to time, usually when we least expect it. It can plunge either of us into a heavily melancholic state, but happily never at the same time. We learn to spot these moments of sadness in each other's eyes and prop one another up while the memory passes.

In December, we have a follow-up appointment with Anthony Kaiser back at St Thomas'. It's lovely to be back on the neonatal unit again with all of our friends – the nurses and doctors who have invested so much in saving the twins. It feels a bit like a victory procession as we sit in the waiting room, receiving a steady stream of visitors, all of whom can't believe how well the twins are looking, 'and how BIG!' We also feel guilty, only too aware that battles are being fought in this unit and that for some families, home is still a distant prospect.

Eventually we wheel the twins into Anthony's appointment room.

'Good morning,' says Anthony, rising from a chair in the corner of the room, his long cricket-like legs unfurling beneath him as he stands.

'Morning,' we chirrup, pleased to see another friendly face.

'All well?' he asks.

'Yes, thanks. You?' I reply.

'I'm well, thank you.' Then straight to business, he begins,

'So this is part of our follow-up programme. We aim to see how well some of our earlier prems are coming on in the world outside of the unit.'

'So far so good,' Georgie says.

'Excellent,' he replies. 'And I understand there have been no visits back to the hospital for respiratory problems.'

'Yes, that's right,' she confirms, beaming proudly. We haven't had much to smile about on the breathing front with the twins, so this success is worth celebrating.

'Well done.' He continues, 'The purpose of today is to undertake some basic tests to see how well the twins are developing intellectually. It's obviously difficult to put them on a normal scale, since they were so premature, but we do need to get a picture of how they're progressing.'

He pauses, to make sure we understand what we're talking about.

'Er, OK,' I say uncertainly, understanding, but not necessarily wanting to.

He explains, 'Well, it stands to reason that the twins won't be following a completely normal path, so we just need to get an idea of how they're getting on.'

There's a pause as he takes in our uncertain faces.

Eventually I ask, 'So, I think we understand that they aren't following a normal route, but doesn't their prematurity mean that they're always going to be a little bit behind their peers in terms of milestones?'

'That's right,' he says, 'but it's also important that we ascertain whether they are also suffering with some sort of global developmental delay.'

Funny terminology, I think to myself, but fair enough.

'So, they're sixteen months now. How have they been doing in general?' he asks.

Georgie says, 'Well, they are understandably some way behind their growth targets at this juncture. Not helped by the reflux and vomiting. It's been hard to get food in and to get it to stay down.'

'And how have they been presenting physically?' Anthony asks.

'Well, no crawling yet,' replies Georgie.

'Are they sitting?' he asks.

'They spend much of their days in their buggies, bouncers and high chairs.'

'Yes, but unsupported?'

'No, not unsupported.'

'How about head control?'

'Very floppy still, their heads often fall forward to their chests when they're upright. Also, the physios have identified some stiffness in both children: arching in the back and neck, some disconnection between their upper bodies and limbs and also stiff hands. We see it more in Alice.'

Anthony says, 'Well, the fact that they are still on oxygen may be a factor. It has an impact on the way that the muscles grow so progress is likely to be slow while Thomas and Alice are still being given air at night. Some of these problems may be related to neurological issues but, equally, they could purely be issues of development which are overcome with time.'

That sounds OK to me. As long as no one is telling me they're disabled, I'm good with that.

'It's hard to get a clear picture about the future until we're past their first birthday, corrected. In other words, past the date at which they should have their first birthday, had the pregnancy gone to full term. So, sometime in the New Year we should be able to get a clearer idea.'

He stops, then continues, 'I'd like to do a simple test with them both. It tests something called object permanence. Object permanence tests our ability to understand whether something still exists, even when it's outside our line of sight.'

'OK?' Georgie says uncertainly.

Anthony wheels a table across to Thomas, who is sitting on Georgie's lap. He then places a red squashy ball on the table. Thomas looks at the ball.

'OK, good,' Anthony says.

He then picks the ball up and holds it in front of Thomas's face. Thomas looks up.

'Does he have a squint?' Anthony asks.

'Yes, I thought that,' replies Georgie.

'OK, it's not unusual for ex-prems to have some difficulty with sight. I'll refer you to the ophthalmologist.'

He then passes the ball from side to side in front of Thomas, who watches it. Anthony then drops the ball below the table out of the line of Thomas's sight. Thomas follows the ball down with his eyes and peers expectantly.

'Good boy,' Anthony says. 'There you go, object permanence. He knows it's still there even though he can't see it.'

He then tries the same test with Alice, with the same result.

The confirmation that there is the presence of some sort of brain power between the twins' ears is very reassuring, and yet all the while, the questions keep coming up in our minds, questions about the their long-term futures.

In the car on the way home, we return to our favourite subject – desperately trying to predict the unpredictable . . .

'Encouraging signs today,' I begin. The twins gurgle happily on the back seat of the car.

'Yes,' Georgie agrees, 'but I don't understand what it all means . . .'

'Hmm,' I mutter.

'What do you think the chances of the twins being normal are?' Georgie says.

'That's a big question,' I reply. 'I don't really know, but I've seen enough from them to feel that they have loads of potential.'

*

Something else has been troubling us through this time. We are becoming increasingly uncertain about Thomas's hearing.

Both twins underwent hearing tests shortly before they left hospital and we were delighted and surprised to learn that all of their tribulations had not had any impact on their hearing.

'That's a very good result,' Anthony told us. 'Extremely premature babies that have a rough start often have complications with their hearing and eyesight later in life, so Thomas and Alice were considered high risk. We were pretty surprised by this outcome, particularly for Thomas, so we ran it a second time just to be certain. He passed the second test too.'

At the time, we were pleased and then forgot all about it, but now we are perplexed by the fact that Thomas does not seem to be responding to sound.

He is sitting on my lap in the kitchen and Georgie walks in behind us.

'Thomas,' she calls.

No reply. No sign of recognition.

'Thomas!' More loudly now.

He sits, looking up at me, seemingly oblivious to her call.

She moves around the room and into his line of sight and he lifts his head to her and smiles.

She smiles back and says to me, 'I think we should get it checked out.'

'Yes, OK,' I reply. 'It may just be delay.' I offer hopefully. 'Glue ear, perhaps.'

'Maybe,' she says. 'But we should do it to be sure.'

*

Soon after our conversation about object permanence with Anthony, we make our way to the office of an osteopath, a man called Stuart Korth. We are keen to see whether his hands might have some positive effect on the twins and we are also keen to seek more medical opinion as it has been hard to get a precise picture. His office is in a large, brick terraced house near Marylebone. There are half a dozen steep steps up to the front door, so we lift the double buggy up to the top.

After a brief discussion about the twins' history and current performance, Stuart explains how his treatment works. 'You'll see me applying very light pressure to the children's head and neck. The idea is to release stresses and tensions from around the body. We find that ex-prems' connective tissues around the head and neck are less well developed so this treatment can provide real benefits. We may also find that the treatment helps to ease some of the tensions in their stomach and therefore improves the reflux.'

'Sounds good,' I reply, just about keeping up.

'Let's get started then,' he says.

He lays Alice down on a bed in the middle of the room. He pulls up a chair alongside the bed and reaches his hands across to her head, feeling with his long fingers around the back of her skull. With tiny, gentle manipulations, he moves his hands quietly and expertly around the back of the head, all the time adjusting and assessing what might be going on inside. He then treats Thomas and after ten minutes says he is finished.

He walks over to a desk in the corner and scribbles some notes before turning back to us to reveal what he has found.

'Let's start with Alice,' he says. 'She has some head control but it seems pretty occasional. I have also noticed that she arches quite significantly. This indicates a deterioration in the control of the muscles in her trunk. Cognitively, she seems a little absent and slow to me.'

It's nothing we hadn't already expected, but the directness of his words come as something of a surprise.

He notes our worried faces and ploughs on.

'Thomas,' he says. 'Here I can see some indications of neural motor developmental issues. He isn't arching as much as Alice and seems more alert but the question persists as to whether he will be within normal limits.'

'What about the future?' Georgie asks.

'It's not that easy to tell, I'm afraid. In the short term, diagnosis is usually clear after one year, corrected,' he replies.

He continues, 'They are part of the same picture. There are indications of some degree of cerebral palsy, but whether this will be clumsiness and stiffness or something more serious is not clear. Having problems with arching and poor neck control would indicate a gloomy prospect so the fact that they have some head control is good news.

'The arching may impact their ability to control their sitting and walking. At the other end, it could just mean that they will simply be clumsy, or curl their toes.'

I latch on to the word 'clumsy' as though it's a life raft. I'm not sure I know what cerebral palsy is, but it doesn't sound too good. Right now, I'll stick to clumsy, I think to myself. Clumsy would be just fine.

Just like their dad, in fact.

*

Spring is soon with us and we are advised to visit a centre called Brainwave in Bridgewater in Somerset, for a three-day physical therapy session.

Brainwave is a charity that teaches disabled kids how to improve their physical capabilities. The hope is that by teaching our children at this stage, they will be given a chance of learning some of the skills that they have yet to gain due to their prematurity.

After the four-hour drive down the M4 and M5, we arrive at a collection of single-storey buildings on an industrial site just off the motorway. We are welcomed by friendly faces and professional-looking staff who seem very familiar with the situation we describe to them as we talk them through the twins' short, but eventful, history on planet earth. It is reassuring to find people who are relaxed about the story we tell and completely comfortable with the ways that Thomas and Alice present.

We begin in a large gymnasium, with small groups of other families. We start with a large padded table in front of us and our physio asks us to take Alice from the chair and place her, face down on the surface of the table.

We duly comply and Alice, as expected, lies flat on the table, her shape like the classic outline of the murder victim marked onto the floor of the room in a police drama: head to the side, one arm up, one arm down and legs out flat behind her.

The physio, Carl, asks Georgie to step up to the table and together they bring Alice onto all fours. Her head hangs down loosely from her shoulders and the only thing stopping her from collapsing flat onto the table are the four hands holding each of her limbs in place.

'You can see she has very low tone,' Carl says.

I thought tone was something musical, I say to myself.

'Yes,' Georgie agrees suddenly. 'Her underlying tone is very low, but from time to time she becomes hypertonic as well, which makes the handling harder.'

I nod a sage nod. Have they noticed the fact that I've got absolutely no idea what they're on about? 'Underlying tone?' 'Hypertonic?' Excuse me?

'It's common with kids with cerebral palsy,' he explains.

I'm still more worried about the fact that Georgie seems to know a hell of a lot more about this than I do. It stands to reason, I suppose. She's spent a lot more time with them and with the physios and OTs, but these are my kids we're talking about! (Must pay attention.)

Carl explains, 'The objective for both babies is to enhance their motor development in a number of different ways. We want to try to enable the upper body and legs to act independently of one another. Walking, sitting and reaching are all facilitated by having the body operate separately from the legs. We'd also like to see better neck and head control. Their arching has caused weakness in the muscles at the back of the neck so we need to try to address that.'

'Yes,' answers Georgie. 'And nine months in the neonatal unit lying flat out can't have helped them there.'

'That's true,' agrees Carl. 'We also want to try to loosen the arms. See how stiff they can be?'

He takes Alice's arm and shakes it to try to help relax the muscles, but her arm remains rigid. Her left hand is balled into a tiny fist and her thumb sticks through between her forefinger and middle finger.

'If we can free the arms up a bit, it will enable the twins to more easily bring their arms and hands in to the middle, and obviously from there they can undertake many more basic tasks with their hands,' Carl explains. 'So, what we do is teach the children how to improve their motor skills through a series of exercises.'

During the course of our visit, we are schooled through various physical activities on the table, designed to help the twins' motor skills improve. Some are exercises where the twins lie prone and we encourage them to open their hands by brushing with different textures, but mostly the exercises involve moving the twins up and down on the padded table, encouraging them to learn how to crawl, for example. We stand either side and lift their legs and arms up and down as we shuffle them along the length of the table. The idea is that over time they will be able to initiate some of these movements themselves.

'You should try to find time to do these exercises twice a day if possible,' explains Carl.

'Difficulty is finding the time,' I say. 'That's two hours of every day when you include both of them and we're still spending eight hours a day feeding them.'

'Yes, I see that,' he allows. 'I realise it's hard finding time for everything, but do as much as you can. It will all be for the best in the long run.'

*

Another day, another specialist.

We are back at St Thomas' Hospital, but this time at the new Evelina London Children's Hospital, which was still being built when the twins were in the neonatal unit, but is now finished. It is a wonderful bright building, with a huge, arched glass atrium which ensures that the hospital is filled with light and life. We have been referred to Dr Jean-Pierre Lin, a neurologist who specialises in kids with motor disorders. Perhaps he can provide us with some clarity?

After some time, we are welcomed by a nurse who takes us into a spacious, bright blue room where we meet Dr Lin. He's slim, well-dressed, in his fifties and has a cerebral but warm manner.

After a brief exchange of niceties and the usual discussion of the twins' medical background and current state of play, Dr Lin asks me to place Thomas onto a physio mat on the floor in the centre of the room.

I unbuckle him from the buggy and lay him on his back on the mat. As soon as he has been put on the floor, he begins pushing through his heels, arching his back and shuffling across the floor. He has a determined look on his face.

I bend down to pick him up, but Dr Lin says, 'No it's fine, leave him.'

Georgie says, 'We've been told not to let him do that by the physios, because it encourages poor posture and arching.'

'Yes,' he replies, 'but I wouldn't worry about him travelling on his back. Sometimes it's about what they can achieve and you can tell he's enjoying getting around under his own steam, however unorthodox. It's motivating for him.'

I like this viewpoint. Clearly this is something that Thomas enjoys and nothing could be more important right now after the horrors of what he has been through.

Dr Lin drops to his knees and rolls Thomas over before pulling him into a crawl position.

'Rolling and time spent on all fours should be encouraged,' he says, pushing Thomas's knees up underneath his chest. 'His legs do not have full range in the hamstrings so you're going to need to work on that.'

He pulls Thomas up into a standing position, supporting him underneath his armpits. Thomas's legs are bowed and he stands on the outside of his feet, hopping from one foot to the other like a drunken sailor dancing the hornpipe.

'It's good that he can support himself on his feet. It's also good that he doesn't cross his legs when he's in this position,' Lin says. 'The abductor muscles at the back of the top of his legs are obviously working. Are you doing standing programmes with them?'

'Yes,' replies Georgie.

The twins' playroom in the basement of our house has recently been filled with all manner of specialist pieces of equipment, the biggest of which are two huge standing frames – large padded wooden devices that we strap the twins into so that they spend a little time each day in supported standing.

This has the positive effect of allowing the muscles and bones in their hips and legs to form more normally.

'You can put him back now,' he says, handing Thomas to me and I return him to the buggy alongside his sister as Dr Lin takes some brief notes. Then he turns and removes Alice's shoes and socks.

'Ah, excellent,' he says. 'You see how her fingers and toes move independently and in a relatively coordinated manner? Thomas too?'

We nod.

'That's encouraging, because it means that their brain signals are reaching the outer extremities of their bodies.'

'So,' he says decisively and it's clear we are about to get his summary. 'The permanence of their condition remains to be seen,' he begins. 'For now, I recommend that you focus on small positive improvements.'

We nod in agreement.

'Dyskinesia is my call. The twins are on the go all the time and have a constant range of movement. This is different from spasticity, which means muscles get stuck in one position.'

I breathe out heavily. Somehow there's something about that word, with all of its pejorative meaning, that I dislike intensely. A flood of relief that it's not a word that Dr Lin thinks applies to our twins.

'I don't personally think that there are any signs of spasticity, but I suspect I'll get letters complaining about that diagnosis!'

We smile. We're with him.

'The good thing about dyskinesia,' he continues, 'is that the development cycle is much longer. With spasticity you get stuck at a certain point. With dyskinesia you keep developing into the tenth year.'

'The fact that we haven't seen any seizures is also a big positive,' he says.

I like this man, I think to myself. Like us, he's focused on the positives.

'A couple of suggestions for you: first, food. They should switch to more solids. It will give them more strength. They have good teeth, so more solids should be possible. It also expands their experiences – choice and variety are very important inputs for the developing brain.'

Georgie nods, she has been campaigning to keep feeding as normal as possible. She says, 'They eat pretty well, though everyone keeps telling us that we need to think about gastrostomies.' These are feeding tubes which are surgically inserted into the abdomen to allow food to be given directly into the stomach.

'Who says that?' he asks.

'Lots of people,' she replies.

'Rubbish,' he says suddenly. 'They always say that for children like yours – but there's no real need. They are not malnourished, look at the pink colour of their skin and their bright eyes. Nonsense.'

This is a minor triumph for Georgie. Feeding them normally is hugely important for us, given that the kitchen table is where all the social action happens in any home. And we know they're sociable.

'Secondly,' he continues, 'you should focus your attention on communication – input is essential from now. . . telling stories, talking, shaping words, providing visual input, tactile input. Get them to face each other and observe each other. But also separate them so they feel individual rather than always travelling together. Sibling competition is already starting at this stage.'

We leave the hospital and both feel encouraged by what we have heard. Some good news, I think to myself.

*

Still we have no clear diagnosis about what the future might bring for the twins and in the absence of anyone telling us otherwise, we continue blithely onwards assuming the best, despite signs pointing us in the other direction.

We are new parents and neither of us has ever lived closely with other children, so we have nothing to compare the twins' progress with.

Privately, we accept that our approach is probably not sensible – we should be preparing ourselves for what might come.

But also part of me thinks, well, if the twins are disabled, we're going to have years to get used to that and deal with it. Why not enjoy this moment of blissful ignorance, when the twins look normal and are small enough to get away with it?

For now, the excuse of their prematurity serves as an ideal cover-up for the multitude of issues that might be lurking beneath the surface. And we carry on, heads held high, supremely confident of a positive outcome in the face of incontrovertible evidence to the contrary.

The honeymoon doesn't last long.

19. Wooden Spoon

It's now a year since the twins came home and Anthony Kaiser has referred us to the Mary Sheridan Centre in Kennington. This is the centre for following up with children who have been born very prematurely and who have suffered difficult early months.

We turn off the main road into the centre and the sign announces 'Mary Sheridan Centre for Child's Health – Wooden Spoon House'.

Interesting branding, I think to myself, not hugely inspiring.

We pull up in the car park, unload the twins into their buggy and walk into the centre for the first time.

It's immediately apparent that the centre is targeted at more than just ex-prems. There's a wide range of kids in the waiting room, all with varying degrees of physical and learning disabilities. There's a Down's kid here, a young boy in a wheelchair whose body seems to be having tremors over there and in the far corner a young girl whose head is the size of mine and who has large goggly eyes.

I'm spooked and shocked by what I see. What are we doing here surrounded by these strange-looking kids? These children are nothing like mine. We sit in the waiting room and do our best not to stare. Looking back to this time in future years, I will be ashamed by the way I used to feel towards kids with disability. But for now, I wonder whether the very fact that Anthony has sent us here means that he's trying to send us a clue as to the potential outcome for the twins . . .

Bury that thought.

The twins' names are called and we wheel the buggy into the appointment room. After half an hour of questions and a further half-hour of physical examination, I begin the line of questioning from which there will be no turning back.

'We're still not clear about the outlook,' I say. 'Over the course of the past year we have been imagining three possible scenarios. The first is that the twins might die. We seem to be beyond that immediate risk now and despite the fact that they are still taking oxygen at night, it seems that we can cross this possibility off the list.'

'The second outcome is that they are disabled in some way. The third is that they are completely fine.'

The paediatrician looks at me quizzically, slightly stunned by the suggestion, and says, 'Well, I think it's pretty evident that you can rule out the last of those options.'

I look at him. That's it then. No more chasing rainbows. The last tiny possibility that they might be normal has been emphatically snuffed out.

*

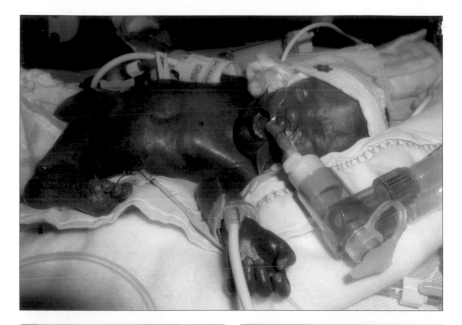

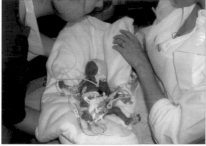

Top: Alice at a day old, no bigger than this page. The stickers along the bonnet are the only reminder that the NICU is a nursery.

Middle: Georgie is allowed to hold Alice for the first time, several months in to her life… Somewhere there's a baby under that tangle of wires and intravenous lines.

Right: Proud Mum and Dad with Thomas at five months old, still so tiny and fragile and we're having to wear aprons and gloves because of his continual infections.

Above left: Home at last... Georgie brings Alice (aged nine months) over the threshold at our new home in Streatham.

Above right: The twins are rechristened once they come home. Thomas seems to be whispering something conspiratorial to his sister.

Below left: Grinning from ear to ear – those smiles always remind us that there's plenty going on inside and that they're enjoying life.

Below right: Thomas blowing out the candles on the twins' second birthday cake.

Above left: Alice loving the unusual sensation of movement during her first riding session.

Above right: Smiling through the pain, Alice with Georgie soon after her eight-hour brain operation. She looks so gorgeous as a baldy!

Below left: With Thomas soon after his second huge head surgery in one year, for his cochlear implant.

Below right: Thomas and I celebrate at the end of the Thame 10k, the fulfilment of sporting dreams for father and son.

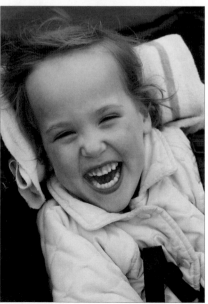

Winning smiles.

It's the middle of the night. Through the fog of sleep, it slowly dawns on me that Georgie is crying.

'George?' I ask.

The sobbing stops.

'George?' I say again.

'Yup,' comes the quiet, strained reply.

'You OK?'

She replies with a sniff.

'I just feel so alone,' she says eventually.

My heart sinks.

'Why?' I ask.

'Because I'm on my own,' she replies. 'You're at work all day and I don't mean that you shouldn't be, I just mean that I'm here on my own with the twins all day. Sometimes, I just need someone to talk to about how I'm feeling and what it's like.'

'The house is filled with strangers, all day, every day, but I can't open up to them, I don't know them,' she continues. 'And there's no one I can call who really understands what this is like. None of my friends have any frame of reference for what's happening to us. They mean well, but they just have no idea what to say.'

I roll over and put my arms around her as if to stress the point that I want to make.

'I'm here, George,' I say. 'We're in this together. Always.'

We lie like that, entombed in the embrace of two people who really haven't got a clue what's coming at them, but knowing that whatever it is, it isn't going to be good.

*

The twins are now almost two and despite plenty of proclamations and viewpoints, we are still no clearer to receiving a definitive diagnosis. We now know that disability in some form will be a feature of these children's lives, but we are no closer to understanding the level of it.

During the following three months, further pieces of the puzzle start to drop into place.

On a visit to my brother's house, I watch my new niece, Isobel, a year younger than the twins, eating her breakfast in her high chair. She is put in the chair and slices of apple are left on the table for her to help herself. She slowly makes her way through the fruit, carefully picking up the pieces and placing them into her mouth.

'Did you see Issey at breakfast?' Georgie says later, when we are alone.

'Eating with her hands?' I reply.

'Yes,' she replies. 'Why can't the twins do that yet? Issey's a year younger.'

'I know, but don't worry,' I reply, unconvincingly. 'Don't forget they've had a rocky start . . . everything is going to take a little longer.'

And then there are the looks from the professionals we come into contact with to assess the twins and discuss their progress. By now we have collected a large gaggle of experts who are intimately involved in the twins' care and daily routines: paediatricians, physiotherapists, occupational therapists, speech and language therapists and so on.

We sit in our living room at home, surrounded by these people at so-called multi-disciplinary meetings and we pretend to ignore the glances they shoot one another when we offer some positive comment about the twins' prospects.

'We're really encouraged by the progress they've made in

the past six months,' I tell them. 'Thomas is really sociable and very focused when he's interested, usually on tasks where he's able to try to use his hands. His feeding is vastly improved; he's chewing and biting quite solid food now and is being sick far less frequently.'

Georgie continues, enthusiastically, 'Also, his hand control seems to have come on well. He's even started giving us high fives!'

'As for Alice,' she continues, 'she seems really bright, really sociable. She loves people and even though she doesn't seem to have any words, she's very vocal so we definitely want to see more input for communication as speech doesn't seem beyond the realms of possibility.'

Just the looks on their faces are enough to tell us that they think we're bonkers to be assuming any kind of positive outcome. But no one says anything. And we pretend not to hear the worried comments they make as they walk away down the path at the front of our house.

We close the door behind them and we are on our own once more. Despite the well-meaning efforts of these people, despite the support of our friends and family, at the end of the day – literally and metaphorically – it comes down to Georgie and me.

We are on our own.

*

Several months later and we are back at Wooden Spoon House. The twins are approaching their second birthday and we feel that it's high time we got a clearer picture about the sort of disability we are dealing with. Are we talking about problems which are going to impact their lives dramatically, or are we talking about minor issues? We had been so stunned at the previous meeting that we hadn't probed any further. Perhaps we'd wanted to, but realised that that was enough to take on in the first instance.

A new doctor, but a similar line of questioning:

'We now know that these children are going to suffer with some form of disability, but we aren't clear how extensive their problems are going to be.'

'Problems', can I say that? Is that allowed? Should I be using the word disability? Is handicapped allowed?

'Can you give us an indication of the severity?' I ask. 'Are we talking about problems that are going to affect just a hand, for example, or something impacting the whole body? We'd like to know whether faculties like speech and walking are going to be possible.'

Once again the look. Different doctor, same incredulous look. A look that says *You stupid boy. How on earth could you ask such a stupid question. Isn't it obvious? Go to the back of the class, you clearly haven't been paying attention.*

She eventually speaks. 'Let me be clear. Thomas and Alice are at the severe end of the spectrum. Their disabilities are profound and will affect them in every aspect of daily living. All four limbs are affected by their disability.'

Silence.

And then, into the silence, these six words...

'They have quadriplegic athetoid cerebral palsy.'

The words smash into my face like a fist. Georgie's face is blank.

'Wha'?' I say stunned.

'What does that mean?' the doctor finishes for me. 'I'm

afraid it means that I don't think these children will ever walk. I don't think there's much hope of them talking either. They will need to be cared for for the rest of their lives. Dressing, feeding, toileting . . . I'm afraid it's a long journey for you both.'

And there, in the pit of my stomach, a primeval dread as I realise that life is about to take a very different course.

*

After the meeting, Georgie and I cling to each other in the car park outside the centre. She cries into my chest and a patch of tears spreads on my shirt. The twins sit in their double buggy in quiet, wide-eyed innocence, oblivious to the sentence that has just been passed down on them. They are a picture of contentedness. I look at them and wonder how the hell we were supposed to be able to tell that it was that serious.

The last time the four of us embraced in a car park it was under very different circumstances – it was the moment of unalloyed joy of having just discovered that Georgie had two tiny lives growing inside her.

Things have come a long way since then.

*

That evening, I spend time on the computer at home looking up these strange words – words that I've never given a second thought to before today. The blue screen of the PC lights the room as I google the words and the NHS website flashes up:

> Cerebral palsy is the general term for a number of
> neurological conditions that affect movement and
> co-ordination.

> Neurological conditions are caused by problems in the brain and nervous system. Specifically, cerebral palsy is caused by a problem in the parts of the brain responsible for controlling muscles. The condition can occur if the brain develops abnormally or is damaged before, during or shortly after birth . . .
>
> The symptoms of cerebral palsy normally become apparent during the first three years of a child's life . . . These symptoms can affect different areas of the body and vary in severity from person to person. Some people only have minor problems, whereas others are severely disabled.
>
> Many people with cerebral palsy also have a number of associated problems, including repeated seizures or fits, drooling problems and swallowing difficulties. . . .

I sit and stare at the screen. I feel numb. The eerie glow of the screen lights my ghostly face.

So this is how it's going to be.

Georgie calls from upstairs: 'Bath time, J! Can you come and give me a hand?'

'Coming,' I reply and step, heavy-hearted, up the stairs to join the three of them – my family.

Thomas is ready for his bath, so I lift him from the bed and carry him through to the bathroom. The bath is already run and I kneel down and lower him into the warm, inviting water. Holding his head with my left hand, I slowly wash the water over his body with my right.

My eyes survey this tiny body – seemingly so perfect, but

evidently so damaged: apparently perfect arms that may never hold me around my neck; perfect-looking legs that may never run, never kick a football; a perfect mouth that may never speak.

As I wash his chest, my tears drip from my cheeks, falling and mixing with the soapy bathwater. Thomas looks up at me and smiles reassuringly.

Thank God someone in this family has got some balls.

20. Grief Encounters

*T*he heavy thump of the bass line reaches everywhere in the club; even into here, in the basement toilets far from the main dance floor and bar area.

I stand at the urinals, and the reassuring thump travels up my spine, bringing a familiar, welcome chill to my neck and making the hairs there stand on end.

'Jimmers!'

Steve slaps me on the back and I spill on my trousers. He grabs my shoulders from behind and lands a smacker on my neck. He comes to stand next to me, smoke from his cigarette spilling up into my eyes and making him squint as he unbuttons his jeans.

'Great night,' I say smiling, my head fogged.

'Great night,' he agrees. *The sense of solidarity of a memorable night shared speaks louder than words and we stand there, smiling, dicks in hand, basking in the glow of the moment.*

A stranger, off his head, barrels into the room behind us,

bellowing the Oasis hit 'Cigarettes and Alcohol', at the top of his lungs.

Steve and I start laughing. He's laughing hard and the smoke from the fag in his mouth is making him choke and now I'm giggling like an idiot as he coughs and splutters, his eyes streaming . . .

*

The alarm clock rings for work and jerks me awake from my dream.

I reach out and press the switch to silence the noise. For a split second, the toasty cocoon of the duvet and Georgie's gentle breathing reassure me that I'm still in a happy place. For that brief moment everything is OK.

Then reality returns to my conscious thought and I realise with dread that that split second of semiconscious comfort is the happiest I am going to feel all day.

*

As I dress, my mind is instantly a whir with all the questions and worries about what the future will hold for the twins, for all of us.

The impact of learning that Thomas and Alice are definitely disabled is a challenge unlike any either of us has faced before. A bomb has gone off in our lives, scattering chaos where once there was order. The smug security of our old lives is shredded as we struggle to reconcile the uncertain future with our comfortable pasts. I think back to my words when they were still tiny babies – 'I don't think I could cope if they were disabled, I think I'd rather they didn't make it' – and I shiver. This is now our reality.

Even though we had survived perhaps the more visceral hour-by-hour routine of those early weeks and months in the neonatal unit, the emotional impact of learning to cope with the twins' disability now feels even more overwhelming.

During those early weeks in hospital, all of our friends and family could see that we were struggling with a life-and-death situation, they could tell that we were exhausted by the endless ups and downs and they were there for us.

The process of learning about the twins' disability is a slow and lonely process. None of our friends have any points of reference or experience to draw on to try to guide and reassure us. Georgie and I are coping alone.

Our community nurse calls and I decide to ask her about these feelings. The crying incident in front of the TV has made me worry about how I'm dealing with everything. She's been through this process many times with other parents and describes this process as being a bit like grieving.

'We tend to think about death when we talk about grieving. But there are also seismic events in one's life that have an equivalent feel to them. In this case it might even be that the process you are going through is worse, as it's not a single event that you rebuild from, it's an ongoing process with many ups and downs, which will continue to influence the way you feel about this.'

Again, I nod sagely and I'm reminded of the young anaesthetist's words just before the twins were delivered.

'You do realise that you are both in for a very long and difficult journey, don't you?'

His words are starting to make sense.

'So you'll find yourself going through these emotions for a

long time, I'm afraid. I don't want this to sound dramatic, but it is a long process. My advice is, seek help if you feel you need it and don't forget to look after yourselves. I've seen it all too often fall apart when the parents take too much on. You are exposed to this and as you have twins so the load is doubled.'

It's hard to pick many positives out of her words. I've never lost a very close family member or friend, so I haven't grieved in earnest before and I can't say whether this feeling feels like the loss of a loved one.

All the same, it does feel like something has been left behind . . .

The dreams for the twins, lost in the space of several seconds as those words were delivered to us. The life that we had hoped for as parents, gone forever.

I spend days thinking this is fine, the twins are lovely and they have a great life ahead of them. And I spend nights lying awake with fright about the future. I'm desperate for the life that the twins will never lead and a sense of loss for the normal relationship that I can never have with them.

And I worry about the future and what it might bring: the realisation that these children will be dependent on us until we are too infirm ourselves to support them. How the hell are we supposed to cope with this? The doctors have passed sentence and now it's our job to just go and get on with it.

But there's no training, no manual, no direction to speak of. What on earth makes them think we have any kind of chance of being able to do this?

*

Mum is on the phone.

been thinking,' she says. 'I think you and Georgie could
th a proper break. Away from the twins, I mean.'

'We've been over this, Mum,' I say, annoyed that we are
once again dealing with an impossible notion. 'I just don't
see how it's possible.' Believe me, I'd like nothing more than
to get away for a few days, it's just never going to be that
straightforward. 'There's too much work involved and you
can't do it,' I say.

'That's fine,' she replies calmly. 'Dad and I have had a chat
about this and he's got a few days coming up in October when
he's not got any meetings. If we can find a nurse to help us
with the nights, then we can manage. I really think you need a
break. Just take a few days, we'll be fine.'

I pretend to be affronted by the suggestion that we need a
holiday so much that we have to hire extra help and get Dad to
clear his diary, but there really is nothing I'd like to do more than
have some time to ourselves. Mum instinctively understands
this. She sees us struggling and knows that we've barely had a
moment to be Mum and Dad. She sees us being carers twenty-
four hours a day and knows that the opportunity to find time
to be husband and wife has been almost non-existent.

Convincing Georgie is less easy – she struggles with the
thought of leaving the twins – but over the course of the next
few weeks we get arrangements in place and before we know it,
the weekend has arrived and Georgie and I are off. We drop the
twins off at Mum and Dad's and then drive the short distance
to the Sun Inn, a pub in Dedham Vale. We have decided to
stay somewhere close to Mum and Dad in case there are any
emergencies.

It's a wonderful, relaxing weekend. The long-forgotten

luxury of lingering breakfasts in bed with the newspaper, soul-enhancing walks through Constable country, alcoholic lunches, afternoon snoozes and three-course dinners in front of roaring pub fires. A chance to be a couple and to talk about dreams and plans, away from the drudgery of caring for the twins.

This is the first time we've been away from the twins since they've been home and I'm worried that switching off will allow everything that Georgie has suppressed over that time to bubble up and bite her on the arse.

Sure enough, after two days of relaxation and lie-ins, it happens and the bubble bursts. There just hasn't been time to think about the enormity of everything until this moment and it's like the cap of a well-shaken bottle of Coke finally being released. Her emotion comes bursting out.

'It never gets any easier,' she cries desperately.

'I know,' I say.

'The loss, the grief,' she says, sobbing.

'People just don't understand that,' she takes a deep, stuttering breath. 'I've never really healed from the beginning, I've never had the chance. And now I just feel alone.'

'You've *got* to take care of yourself, George,' I urge. 'This is a marathon and we have to take better care of ourselves. You in particular.'

Too soon the weekend has passed and we return to my parents with our batteries recharged and hearts topped up with love. Alice bursts into tears when she sees Georgie again and my Mum admonishes her, 'Oh, Alice, come on! You've been fine all weekend!'

Georgie and I lift the twins out of their highchairs and we all settle around the table for a cup of tea.

'So, how's it been?' we ask.

'Fine,' Mum replies. 'Exhausting, but fine.' She smiles reassuringly but looks knackered.

Dad says, 'Funny thing happened on Friday night.' He smiles. 'Oh?'

'I was just checking the twins after they'd gone to bed and Alice vomited all over herself and her cot. I went straight to her and picked her up, made sure her airways were clear and then realised I had nowhere to put her down because the cot was covered in sick.'

'Oh no!' I say.

'So I was going to take her to the bathroom,' Dad continues, 'when I realised that she was still attached to her oxygen supply and that the stupid tube is caught because it's running between the bars of the cot. I couldn't put her down and I couldn't take her out.'

'Ah,' I say, smiling. 'Oh dear. So what did you do?'

'Well, I was a bit stuck, so I called out for Mum,' he says. 'She was crumpled on the sofa in the sitting room, with a glass of wine and the telly on, so she couldn't hear me.'

'Haha! Oh no!' Georgie says. 'So what did you do?'

'Well, luckily I had my mobile in my pocket so I rang the home number . . . no answer.'

'I was exhausted!' protests Mum. 'I couldn't be bothered answering the phone.' She takes over the story now. 'Eventually I started to wonder where he was so I went looking and found him sitting on the floor waiting with Alice.'

'Could've been there all night!' Dad says and we're all laughing, imagining Dad stranded with Alice all night. The twins are smiling at us all.

The break has clearly done us good, even if Mum and Dad do look a bit grey.

*

One weekend a few weeks later and Georgie has gone out for the day. The twins and I are left to our own devices. I love these times, just me with my children, doing it our way. Not necessarily the right way, but our way.

We have reached teatime without major incident. So far, so good! The twins are lined up, side by side in their high chairs and the 'event' that is teatime in our house begins.

I turn to Thomas and lift the spoon to his mouth. His lips remain sealed shut. He's having none of it.

'Shepherd's pie?' he seems to be saying. 'You *must* be joking.'

'Come on, Thomas.' I urge. 'Open up.'

His mouth remains locked shut.

I turn to Alice and put the spoon up to her mouth. Alice begins to shake her head. It's not a deliberate impulse, rather one of her involuntary spasms. Food is smeared across her face by the sudden movement.

I feel my temperature rising. I *have* to get this food into them; they are still so hopelessly small. They must eat. The recent threats of having gastrostomies implanted only add to the pressure.

I try Thomas again, but he's still having none of it. I try to force the plastic spoon through his clenched teeth. He squeals through his teeth in protest. I'm clearly upsetting him and hurting him.

Suddenly Thomas is holding his breath. It's a familiar practice of his when he's distressed or angry. His face turns bright pink.

'Breathe,' I say.

He's purple now and the breath-hold stretches on. The seconds pass by like hours as I wait for him to regain his composure.

'Please, Thomas,' I plead. 'C'mon, take a breath.'

I've seen this many times before, but my heart is once again in my mouth, worrying that this might be the time when he doesn't relent, he doesn't take that all-important breath. His face is now grey, his lips devoid of any kind of colour.

'Thomas!' I shout desperately now, tapping his hand, trying to revive him from the grip of the breath-hold.

His body is shuddering with the effort of it, his back is ramrod straight and head arched back, his eyes rolling back to the back of his head. The plastic baby chair he is sitting in shakes noisily as his body bursts to be freed from its harness.

'Thomas!!'

Suddenly he takes a huge life-giving gasp and his body collapses with relief. He slumps forward in the chair, only the shoulder straps prevent him from falling face first onto the table in front of him.

I know he's OK now, but also that it's unsafe to feed him for a while, so I turn to Alice and lift the spoon to her mouth.

Her head twists away and to the left, facing away from me. I had purposefully sat this side of her as her head often twists to the right, so now I move around to sit on her other side.

I hold her head in a vice like grip to keep her still and try to feed her. Her eyes suggest an increasing panic so I relax my grip. Her head flings out to the opposite side once more and her arm swings up, knocking food across her face and down her front.

'Fuck it,' I exhale heavily. I snap and force her hand down onto the table. Her bottom lip shoots out and she begins to bawl.

'For fuck's sake!' I shout. 'You have to eat!'

The oven door is still open so I turn and kick it closed. The glass shatters instantly.

Now Alice is screaming, terrified by my anger.

What a man. What a prick.

*

The following day, Georgie and I decide to take the twins and the dog for a walk on nearby Streatham Common. It's a beautiful, clear but cold autumn day and so as I put the twins into their buggy in the hallway, I wrap them up warm in fleeces and blankets.

Georgie is coping with the news better than me. She runs up and down the hall stairs, going 'boo!' to the twins and making them jump and giggle with delight. I'm so proud of her for her stoicism and jollity.

The park looks beautiful in the sunshine, the green swathe of grass stretching away up the hill, surrounded by the orange brick of the buildings bordering it. The park is alive with humanity – dog walkers, strollers, kite flyers and footballers.

We walk silently up the hill. At the top, we stop and park the twins' buggy next to a bench. I flick the buggy's parking brake down with my toe and wonder whether this short, almost reflex, action is one I am going to be familiar with all my life. Will they always have wheelchairs?

Georgie and I slump into the bench. I shove my hands deep into my jacket pockets and Georgie links her arm through mine. We look down the hill to the activity below and the view on to London beyond.

At the bottom of the hill football training is taking place, a flurry of activity, several games taking place, with kids as young as five racing up and down their temporary pitches, marked out with small orange cones. The range of different football allegiances is apparent in the bright colours of their strips – red, white, claret and blue – mostly London teams. The shouts from the coaches and players reach us faintly up the hill.

I look at Thomas in the buggy, his legs rendered useless by his disability, and for a moment the contrast strikes me. What if Thomas can never run and compete with his friends? What if the two of us never get to play football together? A strong sense of sorrow rises in me at this thought.

'Are you OK?' says Georgie, noticing the way I'm looking at my son.

'Fine,' I answer.

'Really?' she says.

'Yep, fine.' I smile.

But I'm not fine. I'm grieving terribly for the fact that Thomas and I are unlikely ever to be part of these early-morning kick-abouts.

*

The booze and conversation are flowing. There's a heady glow in my head which comes with friends and alcohol.

It's been a while since we had friends round for dinner and Georgie took some persuading to host a dinner party for eight. We're all new parents and so somewhat inevitably the conversation turns to kids.

'I'm a bit worried about Freddie,' confides one mother.

'Oh, why's that? What's wrong?' asks Georgie, sympathetically.

'He doesn't seem to be hitting his targets,' she replies.

'Oh, what are those?' says Georgie, arching her eyebrows as if to say 'I wouldn't go there if I were you, love.'

'Well specifically his speech,' says the mum, hammering on oblivious to the warning shot Georgie has just fired across her bows.

I look around the table and everyone is listening now, but I seem to be the only one who has recognised the dangerous ground we are entering.

'Yeah,' starts Freddie's dad. 'Lots of his friends are speaking quite well and even starting to build sentences, but Freddie doesn't seem to be able to say more than a few words.'

'Oh dear,' says Georgie, looking down at her plate and absently twisting her pasta around her fork.

'We're worried he might get left behind when he starts school,' says the mum. 'I mean he's nearly two and he should really be doing better.'

Georgie glances up at me and I shake my head slowly, imperceptibly to anyone else around the table. I can tell she's thinking exactly what I'm thinking. The temptation to burst into a tirade is strong.

It requires a huge effort not to say it. We both know why we stay quiet. Not because we don't think that everyone would benefit from hearing it, we stop ourselves because we are having a nice time and these are our friends.

To say it would be to roll an unpinned, social hand-grenade across the table which would leave the evening – and quite possibly some friendships – in tatters.

So we nod and coo sympathetically.

'Who'd like some pudding?' trills Georgie with a perfect hostess smile on her face.

I love this woman.

*

One thing we do know is not to look too far ahead. For example, we have the immediate challenge of choosing the right path for school when we don't yet have a clear idea about their capabilities.

'Do we go mainstream or special needs?' I ask.

'I just feel that we keep things on a normal path for as long as possible,' Georgie replies. 'Until we have certainty about just how disabled they are, I just feel that we should continue to aim for the best. We should give them as much normality as possible.'

Not for the first time, I agree with her and her boundlessly positive targets for the future.

'I've found a lovely little pre-school in Brixton, called Maytree. It's mainstream, but they say they can take the twins as well,' she continues.

'Let's take a look,' I agree. 'Perhaps we can do a few days there as well as the day at Small Steps?'

Small Steps is a nursery for kids with developmental delay and motor disabilities in Roehampton, South London. The school uses the principles of conductive education – a structured programme which incorporates physical skills alongside learning skills. It has been a great success to date.

The combination of mainstream and specialist settings seems like a perfect hedge for me, while we adapt to this new world and recalibrate our own expectations for the future.

*

Given the good things that Georgie has been saying about Small Steps, I'm eager to see it for myself. A few weeks later I take a day off work to come and see what the fuss is all about.

We arrive at a small, single-storey brick building in Roehampton, unload the twins from their car seats and put them into the double buggy, which we then wheel in through the glass double doors.

We enter the therapy room and unload the children onto the soft mat in front of us. We line up along the mat in a row, about a dozen of us, each parent or carer with a small child sitting in front of them. Most of the kids here seem to have cerebral palsy and to have similar patterns to our twins.

We are greeted by Anthea Pell, the leader of the session. She is tall, slim, bespectacled and, as always, smiling. Once we are all gathered, Anthea begins the session with a welcome song.

'Hello, hello, how are you?' we sing. Each child is greeted in this manner.

Thomas is seated on the mat in front of me and Georgie is sitting alongside me with Alice between her legs. She is belting out the words and waving Alice's arms in the air in time to the words. Alice is beaming, enjoying the sound and the motion as her turn comes around. We then take the children through a variety of stretches and hold them in various positions to encourage them to bear their own weight, through their arms, much like at Brainwave. The objective is to try to develop the strength – particularly their core strength – through their trunks and necks, but also through weight bearing through their arms.

After half an hour of stretching, Anthea hands around a

large container of various sensory items – balls with rubber spikes, feather boas, a scarlet afro wig and other things for the children to feel. We brush the items up and down their arms and place them under their hands to help the children to feel the contrasting sensations of each article.

Georgie takes a bright pink feather boa and wraps it round her neck. Then she dons the afro and starts shaking her head from side to side. It wobbles as she sways from side to side, pulling her face into ape-like grimaces and contortions.

Thomas's nose wrinkles and his cheeks rise as he starts to enjoy the show being put on for him by his mother. Alice's face lights up with a huge, beatific smile. The twins love nothing more than a bit of slapstick.

The twins begin laughing properly now, giggling like banshees. Thomas's shoulders shake with amusement.

The session ends and we are offered coffee and a chance to mill around and meet the other parents. We chat to a mum who is there with her gorgeous daughter. Her girl seems much more capable than the twins, with speech and hand control and a pretty, smiling face. Even so, her mother seems on edge.

'I just don't know what to do with her,' she admits to Georgie. 'I just can't find the energy to be with her and entertain her all the time, so I tend to just put her in front of the telly, because I don't know what else to do.'

In the car on the way home, we discuss this brief conversation.

'It's so sad,' Georgie says. 'That little girl has so much about her, so much going on.'

'I know,' I agree.

'But she's not going to flourish in front of a TV all day.'

'Hmm,' I say. Then, 'We're so bloody lucky to have you, George.'

'Why?' she asks.

'Because you make it all such fun for the twins,' I reply. 'You fill their days with laughter.'

'I just feel that if I can make them smile every day, I will have done my job,' she replies. 'That's all I'm looking for. Just a smile from each of them to let me know that they want to be here, that we did the right thing keeping them alive.'

*

On the eve of the twins' third Christmas, things take a sudden turn for the worse for Thomas. And when the shit hits the fan, I'm in the most unhelpful place I can be – on the golf course – with my phone switched off. Now I'm not much of a golfer. The petty rules and misogynies involved in the game have always served as something of a deterrent. To say nothing of the fact that I've always been unimaginably crap at it.

However, on Christmas Eve, in the comfortable bosom of my family up in Suffolk, the opportunity to take a few hours off from looking after the twins, to wander round a course with my dad, brother and brother-in-law is too good to pass up. Especially as Mum, Georgie and my sister have everything under control back at Mum and Dad's. Both Mum and my sister Emma have proved extremely capable with the twins, throwing themselves into their care with love and fun, despite the unfamiliarity of it all.

After a round of golf, where the conversation is many times more entertaining than the golf, we return to the clubhouse for a not particularly well-earned pint. Dad switches his phone on and immediately it rings.

He answers it.

'Oh, hello, darling,' he says.

He's quiet for some twenty seconds while the voice on the other end speaks, loudly and urgently.

'Right,' he says, calmly, uncertainly, suddenly looking concerned, looking at me. 'Let me put him on.'

He hands the phone to me. 'It's Emma,' he says.

'Hi, Jass,' she begins, and hurries on as I greet her back. 'It's Tommy. He's had to go to A & E.'

She sounds shaken.

'Oh, what's happened?' I ask, a familiar tingle of dread up my spine.

'He stopped breathing, so we called an ambulance. Georgie's gone with him in the ambulance to Colchester Hospital. You need to get there as quickly as possible.'

'On my way,' I say.

By the time I reach the hospital and locate Thomas's bed space, things seem to have stabilised. Thomas is breathing again and seems calm.

Georgie, however, is shaken by what's just happened and she fills me in on the previous two hours.

'The twins were having their afternoon nap and just by chance I happened to be walking past their room and I heard a strange sound. I went in and Tommy's eyes were open but he wasn't focused at all. He was making a very odd noise.' She makes a guttural clicking sound from the back of her throat.

'He'd stopped breathing, so I tried to rouse him, but nothing . . .' She trails off, obviously shaken by the recollection of this frightening moment.

'I called Emma and your mum and they rang 999. They sent an ambulance and stayed on the phone and talked us through what we should do, putting him in a recovery position and trying to get him breathing again.'

'By the time the ambulance arrived he was recovering, but they said to bring him in anyway to have him checked over properly.'

'Jesus,' I say. I feel so small, so embarrassed that I was in the wrong place while all this was going on. 'Sorry I wasn't there for you, George.'

I wrap my arms around her and she rests her head against my shoulder.

'Do you think we can bring him home today?' I ask hopefully. I want, more than anything, for us to be together as a family on Christmas morning.

'The doctors say to keep him here overnight,' she replies. 'I'll stay with him, J. You have a nice Christmas Eve with your family.'

Two Christmases out of three in hospital since our family started. How shit is that? I think to myself. It's a painful, poorly timed reminder of just how vulnerable our children are.

*

At 5 a.m. on Christmas morning, Alice wakes early and I bring her into my bed. I'm still half asleep so I doze as I hold her close to my chest. Every so often I open my eyes and she is there, smiling. She seems to think that my closing and reopening my eyes is some sort of game. Her eyes are like saucers and her pink cheeks are rosy with the heat that our bodies are generating together beneath the duvet.

Her hand, which we have been told will always be incapable of any form of direction, seems to be exploring the contours of my face. She splays her usually fisted hand open and touches my face tenderly. Her legs scrabble beneath the duvet and her back starts to arch backwards with the effort of directing her hand.

Her eyes are wide with excitement as she does so and I lie, thrilled by the thought that this might be a deliberate movement, a concerted attempt to use her hand.

For a split second, in this moment, I forget the doctor's words and she is perfect again, just as she was in the moments before she was born . . . on the same path, the same trajectory, as every other baby in its mother's womb.

21. Curing the Incurable

'There's no cure for cerebral palsy.'

So begins the section on treating cerebral palsy on the NHS website.

Tchk. What do they know? What do they know with their armies of paediatricians, physiotherapists, occupational therapists, neurologists? What do they know with their decades of experience? What do they know, having been through the process of seeing children grow up with cerebral palsy countless times?

With the responsibility of becoming a parent of disabled kids comes the responsibility of feeling that we must try absolutely everything we can to give them a chance.

They are three years old now. We understand that the twins will most likely never walk. We get it. But, totally illogically, we also know that we have to try everything we can to allow that to happen. Even if it's a 0.00001 per cent chance, we have to try it.

The same goes for hand control, for speech, for eating, going to the loo: all of the basic functions that we all take for granted. The only certainty is that if we don't try, they will never do any of these things.

Which is how we how we end up undertaking a flurry of therapies and courses to try to help the twins: physical therapies, alternative therapies, kinetic activities and even spiritual activities.

Some are standard and traditional.

Some are downright bonkers.

We try them all.

We have to.

*

We return to Bridgewater, back to Brainwave, for an assessment and catch-up on progress. In addition to the physiotherapy that they practise at the centre, they also do music therapy and we are keen to see whether this might have an effect on the twins.

Soon after arriving, we make our way to the music room and are greeted by a kindly woman. We explain the background to her.

'The only thing to mention is Thomas's hearing,' says Georgie. 'We think he might not be hearing as well as he should, so I don't know what his response will be to the music. It will be interesting to see.'

'That's no problem,' she replies. 'Even the resonance of some of the instruments can be a powerful source of healing.'

'OK, great,' says Georgie. 'I just don't feel he's responding well to sound, even quite loud ones.'

'OK,' she responds. 'Music has a funny way of slicing through much of the trauma that young children like Thomas and Alice have suffered. Children who go through such life-threatening events tend to wrap a protective blanket around their cores to stop anything bad getting in. As the traumas continue, the protective layers increase – like the layers of an onion – so that it becomes increasingly difficult to penetrate to their core, their soul, the very essence of their being.'

I'm just about following this.

'So the result is that these children become very introspective, very closed to the world around them and they retreat into their shell.'

I realise that these are some of the signs that Thomas, in particular, has been displaying of late. He seems to exist in his own tiny bubble sometimes, very occasionally lifting his head to deliver a killer smile, but mostly just existing in a world of his own.

'Let's get started, shall we?' she says and pulls a guitar out.

OK, here we go, smile and join in.

She starts to strum and Alice immediately smiles and watches her intently. Thomas is smiling too, especially when he's given the chance of strumming the strings himself.

'Let's try the sound board,' she says after a while.

She lays down a large wooden board, one metre square and slightly raised from the floor. She then produces a cello, positioning the point of the instrument on the corner of the board.

'Put Thomas on the board,' she says.

I lift him down onto the board and lay him on his back. He immediately starts wriggling and pushing through his heels, expressing either a lack of comfort or a desire to move himself off the board. I lean forward to stop him from pushing himself off the edge, but the music teacher stops me, saying, 'It's OK, leave him for now.'

She pulls the bow across the strings of the cello and a wonderful sound emanates and a deep resonance fills the room, spilling upwards from the vibrations on the board and through the floor.

Thomas stops wriggling almost immediately, seemingly entranced by the sound and reverberations shuddering through his tiny body. His face, arms, legs and body are all completely still as he enjoys this unfamiliar sensation. He begins to smile and appears momentarily lost in the sensation and vibrations of the music.

'Well,' I announce triumphantly. 'I think we can safely say that rules out Thomas being deaf.'

Hubris, as I will later discover, is an unseemly and deeply unhelpful state of mind.

*

Boosted by the success of the musical experiment at Brainwave, we connect with my Aunt Sally, who has been practising a revolutionary new sound therapy from her home in Lewes, Sussex.

This treatment is a sensory sound therapy which can correct certain brain malfunctions – depression, musical tone, physical and learning problems – and Sally has very generously offered to come up to our London home and lend us the equipment, with two sets of headphones for the coming weeks.

'It's all about energy,' she explains to me in her gruff baritone over the phone. 'Some kids who have early births end up with learning difficulties because the brain was damaged at or just after birth.'

So far, so familiar.

She continues, 'The therapy works on the plasticity of the brain, especially the neural circuits involved in the decoding and analysis of sounds, as well as on those involved in balance and coordination.'

'Sure,' I say, although I'm anything but sure of how on earth it's supposed to do that. In for a penny . . .

'So it teaches children to develop strategies to deal with and manage their learning difficulties and language disorders. It won't eliminate their problems altogether, but it does help the person manage them better.'

Sally is my dad's stepsister, a musical, entertaining fireball of love and energy and all-round badass. She has just set up with a young heroin addict who is half her age and who has recently been released from prison. My dad has therefore given me strict instructions not to supply her with any money if she asks for it.

We love her for her alternative attitudes, her disrespect for authority and in spite of her tendency to come careering off the rails in spectacular fashion from time to time. And we love her because of the way she has dedicated herself to her disabled son, Luke, who is now in his twenties. Luke has very little in the way of speech, but he loves unconditionally and his hug is one of the most joyful, unbounded experiences as he squeezes you half to death. He is permanently hungry and prone to occasional bouts of nodding rage if food is not immediately forthcoming.

'Luke and I look forward to seeing you,' she says.

'It will be lovely to see you both again,' I reply and we say our goodbyes, Sally signing off with her usual 'Hugs.'

They arrive like a couple of hand grenades being rolled through the front door. Sally barrels in with her usual flourish, smothering us all with her huge hugs, love and her unique energy. Luke comes in behind her and swallows us up with even bigger hugs, before he starts to pace up and down shaking his head and pointing to his mouth.

'In a minute, Luca,' Sally tells him and we settle into our living room. After a short while of catching up and introductions to the twins, she starts to talk us through the technology.

'Sound is transmitted to the brain in two ways – through the ear and by bone conduction caused by a vibration in the upper part of the cranium. So you see the headphones also have a little speaker at the top here which sits on top of the skull to send vibrations directly to the brain. We have developed sounds specifically to trigger a reflex in the brain, designed to energise the neural pathways that carry sound around the brain.

'Let's try the headphones on,' she says.

She plops the huge headphones onto Thomas's tiny head and we all start laughing: he looks ridiculous and the headset is sliding around his head and down over his face.

Georgie fetches a headband and secures the headphones in place and asks, 'Is it OK if we do the therapy while they're having their afternoon nap? That's probably the best way to keep the headphones on.'

'Yes, that's fine,' replies Sally. She stands back and looks at Thomas. 'Perfect!' she says. She then looks at Georgie and at me, before saying, 'You two look knackered.'

Georgie smiles and then says, 'It's a lot of work . . . as you know.'

'It certainly is,' says Sally. 'How are you coping?'

'Depends whether you want the scripted answer or the real one,' I say, smiling. She knows only too well what I mean.

'In truth, it's hard to adjust,' I say, knowing full well that she, more than anyone, doesn't need it dressing up. 'It's not at all what we expected and there's absolutely nothing that can prepare you for what's involved in looking after kids like this – the physicality of the role, the drudgery of caring for them, the exhaustion of endless sleepless nights and the fact that you have to constantly think on their behalf as well as your own.'

She nods. She knows.

'It's all of the things that every parent of a newborn has to worry about, but it lasts forever,' she says.

'Exactly,' says Georgie. 'And more. Are they comfortable? Are they facing the right way? What game do they want to play? How can you tell what game they want to play? Do they need a drink? Are they wet? Have they had their medicine?'

'Knackering,' admits Sally. 'And all the while you're dealing with the shattered dreams of not having the child you were supposed to have.'

We nod and then Sally says, 'Have you read the piece by Emily Perl Kingsley? "Welcome to Holland", it's called.'

I look at George and then seeing her blank face say, 'No, I don't think so.'

'You'd remember it if you had,' Sally says. 'She had a son with Down's and she wrote a piece on what it is like to bring up a disabled child. She compares the excitement of expecting a baby to that of going away on a holiday to Italy, glamorous Italy full of history and art. You have bought the guidebooks, made plans, learnt a few Italian phrases . . . but when the baby is born – when the plane lands – you are not in Italy, you are in Holland – and there you have to remain.'

'OK?' I say, not yet following.

Sally notes my quizzical expression and says, 'The point is, you're not in a horrible place, though, just a different one – you have to buy new guidebooks, learn a new language . . . and after a while you begin to notice all the positive things that Holland has to offer . . . tulips, windmills and even Rembrandts.'

'I see,' I say, finally cottoning on.

'She does not pretend it's all great,' Sally continues. 'There are all the people who went to Italy who talk earnestly about what a great time they had there and she says that the pain will never, ever, ever, ever go away. But I think her last line says, 'If you spend your life mourning the fact that you didn't get to Italy, you may never be free to enjoy the very special, the very lovely things – about Holland.'

'Cool,' I say.

'Where's Luke?' Georgie suddenly asks.

We rush to the kitchen where Luke has found the biscuit barrel, the chocolate drawer and the crisps cupboard. It's a scene of devastation – empty packets and half-eaten food everywhere.

'No, Luke!' says Sally. 'Oh God, I'm sorry.'

'Please don't worry – it couldn't matter less,' Georgie says.

At this Luke envelops Georgie in a big bear hug, relieved not to be in trouble.

'Aah, thank you, Luke,' Georgie says.

He hugs her tight and hangs on, and on, and on. Georgie is starting to look a bit squashed and short of breath.

'OK, thank you, Lukey,' she says again, trying to disentangle herself.

'We should be going,' Sally says. 'Come on, Luke.' At this he drops his arms and follows his mother obediently towards the kitchen door.

'Oh, please don't worry,' I say, but they're off through the hall towards the front door.

Sally and I hug at the front door and she says, 'Sorry to ask, but is there any chance I could have a tenner? We need some petrol money and money for Luke for food?'

My father's words ring in my ears.

I pull out a twenty and thank her for coming and for lending us the kit. We wave the car off and turn to close the front door.

Georgie puffs her cheeks out.

'Phew!' I say.

'He's eaten a whole slab of cheese as well,' says Georgie. 'Looks like your macaroni cheese is going to be just macaroni tonight!' and we both burst out laughing.

The tornado has lasted all of ten minutes.

*

Mum has told us about a church in Sussex where they practise healing with a laying-on of hands. Like us, she is determined to not to leave any stone unturned.

For me, the question of faith is not a straightforward one. On the one hand, someone up there seems to have dealt us a pretty uneven hand. On the other, the memories of Thomas's third night, when his baptism seemed to save his life, are as fresh today as they were back then. God knows we could do with another miracle.

We look it up on the Internet:

The Church's ministry is the continuing work of Jesus Christ, who seeks to heal a broken world and broken lives. His purpose is one of wholeness, within ourselves and between us and God. We seek to be instruments of his healing purpose in our care for the whole person, through our medical, counselling and pastoral skills and above all through our prayerful seeking of the guidance and power of the Holy Spirit.

Um, well, OK then.

Several weeks later we drive through the Sussex woods to a beautiful manor house deep in the countryside. We join the congregation at the back of the nearby church and soon the service begins.

After a short while, we are invited to the front, where the vicar takes turns laying her hands on the twins' heads and sending up a prayer and a blessing. The twins both smile, serenely, apparently oblivious to the extraordinary miracle that just might be being passed down through the palms of the vicar.

The vicar lifts her hands from the twins' heads.

Both twins spectacularly fail to leap up out of their buggies and onto their feet. Neither of them looks any more likely to jump up and do a cartwheel than they did before.

Later, we eat a picnic on the rolling lawn at the front of the house. I take Thomas into my arms and roll down the green bank of the lawn. He giggles contagiously as he's tumbled like clothes in a washing machine, down to the bottom of the bank.

*

CURING THE INCURABLE

After several months of trialling the Brainwave techniques and Aunt Sally's equipment, it is hard to see any discernible improvements.

Two hours of every day are given over to helping the twins to move their bodies up and down the soft-topped table that Brainwave has provided us with. The process is arduous and repetitive, but that's exactly what it is supposed to be. The repetition is teaching the twins muscle memory and as for it being arduous –well, who said parenthood was going to be easy?

As long as we keep moving, keep trying things, we continue to believe that we have a chance of winning. Don't stop. Never stop. If we stop, we might be confronted by the futility of our efforts and the inevitability of our future and that might just prove too much to take.

Someone out there somewhere has the solution that is going to make the twins' lives so much easier. We just need to keep looking.

And before long, what looks like the perfect answer lands on our lap.

*

Aunt Sally tells us about a treatment that has been developed by a friend of hers, Linda, for her teenage son, who has cerebral palsy. This treatment has had a profound effect on her son, to the extent that he is now walking and talking. She has commercialised the treatment and has families flocking to her centre in East Grinstead to learn the therapy so that they can continue with it at home.

After briefly consulting her website, we decide to give it a try, and several weeks later, we are in Linda's centre, learning about the Scotson treatment.

She greets us as we arrive. She has an earthly quality, which soothes our apprehension immediately and also explains how she and Sally came to be friends.

Linda ushers us into a meeting room and we sit alongside the twins in their double buggy as the now familiar line of questioning begins. 'So, tell me about the twins. Tell me where they're up to developmentally.'

'Well,' starts Georgie. 'For some time, it was difficult for us to get any kind of proper diagnosis, but things are starting to become clearer now.'

'How old are the twins now?' she asks.

'They're three.'

'Corrected?'

'No, three including the four additional months caused by their prematurity.'

'Ok, and where are they up to?'

'They can't walk. They can't crawl. They don't sit unsupported. They don't have sufficient head control to be able to hold their heads up a lot of the time. Thomas has recently started shaking and banging his head. He also has a squint, as you can see.'

Georgie turns Thomas's head towards Linda, who leans in and nods.

'Speech?'

'No. Good, loud voices but again no discernible words.'

'OK. Tell me about their breathing.'

'Obviously given his history, Thomas's lungs aren't in brilliant condition and they both have chronic lung disease. Thomas's breathing seems worse than his sister's, he often sounds bunged up, and he also has a tendency to hold his breath for long periods when he gets frustrated. Alice's lungs seem OK now, although she took much longer – about eighteen months – to come off oxygen altogether. Her reflux has also pretty much disappeared.'

'What do the doctors say about their prospects?' she asks.

I can see Georgie start to wobble, so I say, 'Quadraplegic athetoid cerebral palsy. Thomas's trunk is weak, his head control is OK and his patterns are largely flexor.' I'm starting to get the hang of the terminology now. 'His limbs are particularly stiff and he is resistant to people manipulating them. However, he does have some capacity to control his arms and hands – for example he can take his dummy from my hand and put it in his mouth. He usually beams with delight once he has done it.'

'Alice has significant issues with her gross motor control,' I continue, 'and is badly affected by persisting asymmetrical tonic neck reflex, which makes her head swing to the side when she wants to look forwards. This prevents her from doing almost anything with her hands, though we believe that we are starting to see some improvements on this front. When she is very interested in something, usually the TV or the dog, she holds her head well, but otherwise has problems with head control. Her pattern is typically extensor and she arches ferociously and this is usually allied with tongue thrusting.'

I realise that I've been avoiding the question.

Eventually I say, 'The specialists tell us that they will never walk, talk or be able to live independent lives.'

'And what about you? What do you think?' Linda asks.

This is an unusual line of questioning for us. What we think hasn't really come in to it.

'I think they're probably right,' replies Georgie and her eyes fall to the floor. My heart snaps to hear her admit it.

'Tell me what they can do,' Linda says, smiling kindly.

Georgie brightens immediately, as though a switch has been flicked. 'Well there are things we know they can do and there are things we think they might be able to do in time . . . Things like a degree of hand control, a bit of speech . . . They understand a lot, you know.'

'What about the things you know they can do?' says Linda.

'They smile, they laugh and they love,' replies Georgie, smiling herself now.

Linda returns the smile.

'Which, when you think about it,' Georgie continues, 'is actually quite a lot.'

*

Later, Linda explains the theory behind the treatment. 'Our therapy is all about enabling brain-damaged children to learn to breathe well. Getting it right can have a profound impact on many other important functions.'

She continues, 'When a child has sustained early brain damage, like the twins, breathing is affected in many ways. From what you've already told us, the twins had lots of lung problems in hospital.'

We nod in well-practised unison.

'You can tell they were premmies, just by looking at them,' she continues. 'See how flat their rib cages are? And Alice in particular has a premmie head, long and thin. A bit like a horse.'

Oh, I think disappointedly, having rather ambitiously

assumed that Alice was by far the most beautiful girl ever to have been born.

'This all happens because the twins are removed from the uterus so early. At a time when they should be snuggled safely inside Mum's tummy in the foetal position, they are laid flat out in an incubator and gravity has its effect as their bodies are still developing and the bones still forming.'

'Breathing is such an important function and not just in the way that we all tend to think of. It affects posture, chest structure, circulation, chewing, swallowing, speech, body weight and many other things.'

Interesting, I think to myself, many of the functions that the twins are struggling with.

'Every cell in the body is dependent on oxygen to function properly. These cells make up tissue and tissue makes up organs, including the muscles and the brain. Normal breathing plays an important role in the creation of normal structure and growth, and supplies critical levels of oxygen to the developing brain and nervous system.'

She pauses to check we are following. We are. This is fascinating.

She sums up, 'Which is why breathing well is so important to help these kids achieve their full potential.'

On the wall she has an array of photographs of children who have gone through the treatment, a photo before and one after. She points out the improvements that the children have made through the process – a straighter spine here, a stronger chest there. We lean in to the photos and strain to see the improvements.

After the meeting, we repair to a side room, where other

parents and their children are sitting, in order to feed the twins their lunch.

A mother and her disabled daughter are in there. The daughter seems, to all intents and purposes, to be entirely lifeless. She has no movement, her mouth hangs open and she stares into nothingness. We begin talking to her mother.

'She was a perfectly happy and healthy three-year-old until last year,' she explains. 'We had a terrible accident last summer. She fell into a full swimming pool and cracked her head on the side as she fell in. It was a while before we found her, floating face down in the water. The ambulance saved her life, but the damage that was done to her brain has been terrible. She doesn't show any signs of recognition – even me – and she can't move a finger.'

We shake our heads, stunned by the horrendous sequence of events that this mother has been through – the horror of the moment that they found her daughter in the pool and the subsequent succession of bad news that would have followed after her life was first saved.

I look across at Thomas and Alice and suddenly feel very guilty about feeling bad about our situation. Our beautiful beaming children are a joy to behold – not just for us, but for everyone who comes into contact with them – and there isn't a day that doesn't go past when the twins don't say, 'I love you, Daddy,' with their eyes and smiles.

I'm beginning to realise just how lucky we are.

*

In the afternoon our formal tutelage in the Scotson technique begins. We lift Alice out of the double buggy and put her onto a flat surface. Thomas sits alongside the vacated space and wonders what's about to happen.

Not very much is the short answer, Tommy.

'You fold the flannels like so,' says our tutor, picking up a flannel from the table and shaping it into a sausage. 'And then gently, but firmly press the flannels against her chest – here, here and here. Two minutes of compressions on each point and then move onto the next.'

Georgie looks at her. She's too polite to say, 'Is that it?' but I can tell that's what she's thinking.

So she starts. Pressing, gently but firmly, here, here and here.

And then it's my turn. 'Firmly but gently,' I say and Georgie suppresses a giggle.

*

In the car on the way home, we discuss the day's experience.

'I really think this could be it,' I say. 'This could be the one treatment that makes all the difference.'

'Yes,' Georgie agrees.

'Did you see Linda's son? Walking around and talking with everyone.'

'I know, amazing, apparently the doctors gave him no chance of ever doing those things,' Georgie says.

'Wouldn't it be amazing if our twins walked,' I say.

'Let's keep dreaming,' says Georgie.

*

We return home invigorated by the possibilities of the Scotson therapy and committed to making a difference using this new treatment.

Two hours a day are given over to it. Georgie and I take it in turns to stand beside the twins' cots as they sleep during their afternoon nap. Georgie's oldest friend, Ben, who runs an oyster import business, has even given up an afternoon a week to come and help us with it. He arrives in a white van and overalls, smelling like Unhygienix from the *Asterix* cartoons.

We start with the lower left chest, thirty seconds of compressions, up down, up down, slowly, gently. Then we move to the middle of the left chest, again thirty seconds, up, down, up, down. And then the top of the rib cage. Another thirty seconds.

And repeat.

Three times.

Then on to the right-hand side.

And repeat.

Three times.

Then on to the twins' backs.

Etcetera.

Etcetera.

Et-bloody-cetera.

*

It's late. Georgie and I are coming to the end of another weekday. I'm knackered, slumped on the sofa watching mindless TV when Georgie puts her head around the door.

She says, 'J? Please can you make the meds up for the twins for tomorrow morning?' and she quickly disappears around the corner to continue with her tasks.

'Always me,' I mutter under my breath, assuming, incorrectly as it turns out, that she is out of earshot.

'What was that?' she calls from the hallway outside the sitting room.

'Nothing,' I reply. Shit.

'What did you say?' Georgie re-enters the room. She looks like she might be ready for a fight.

'Why do I always have to do the meds?' I say. 'I've got an early start tomorrow and need to get to bed.'

Georgie looks at me, disbelievingly.

I relent. 'OK, I'll do them, but on the condition you come to bed. You're always so late coming to bed nowadays. You look tired.'

Now this is just disingenuous and plain selfish. There's only one reason why I want her to come to bed and it has nothing to do with my concern for her well-being.

'I can,' she says, 'but I also have an early start tomorrow, as you know. And I don't have the luxury of being able to go to bed now as I've got a to-do list as long as my arm before I can even think about a bath.'

'Don't exaggerate.' I snip.

'Don't exaggerate?!' She exclaims. 'Would you like me to run you through my list?' She stands brandishing a piece of paper, which, to be fair, looks like it might have quite a lot of tasks on it.

And she's off . . .

'First up I have to do the payslips for the carers so that everyone gets paid this month. Then I need to fill out the tax return for them. When I've done that I need to email the wheelchair service for a new headrest for Alice's buggy. I spent half an hour on the phone with them today and still no one seemed to be able to sort out the relevant part so I've had to photograph it and email it in.'

'Then I've got to reply to the architect about getting these adaptations done downstairs. They can't do anything until we send them measurements.'

'After that, I need to order new special inserts for the twins' boots. As you know, they've been getting blisters on their toes because they curl when they're in their standing frames, so we need some inserts to hold their feet in place.'

I stare at the floor embarrassed.

'Next on the list? SEN statements. Christ knows how long that's going to take me. It's a thirty-page form – one for Alice, one for Thomas. Plus all of the supporting letters from the community team that I need to arrange to send in with it.'

'I've got Social Services coming around tomorrow. They want to reduce the hours of care we are currently receiving due to budget cuts. I need to prepare what I'm going to say to them to convince them to leave things as they are. We're desperately short on help as it is.'

I'm feeling smaller and smaller.

'Then I have a letter to write to a charity that the OT mentioned who we need to ask to fund the twins' Second Skin suits.'

'And, last, but by no means least, the twins' packed lunch for a school trip tomorrow.'

She stands, holding the list up in front of her, trembling with anger.

'So, if I ask you please – pretty please, with a fucking cherry on top – to take five minutes to do the meds, I would really appreciate it,' she says.

We look at one another. Georgie's eyebrows arch as she looks at me expectantly. We're like two boxers circling one another in the ring, both reluctant to make the next move for fear of the consequences that it might bring.

'Why didn't you do all those things earlier in the day?' I ask. The question's out before I can even think about how stupid that sounds.

'Er, I don't know, J? Probably something to do with feeding the twins, doing their baths, doing their Scotson therapy, seeing the OT, their hospital appointment. I know you think it's easy for me because I don't have to go to work every day, but the reality is something different.'

She stops.

Then suddenly she says, 'I haven't had a pee all day. God, I need a pee,' and she's rushing to the door.

I'm grateful I don't have to answer to that tirade. I feel like such a twat.

Being a mother . . . fuck that shit.

*

The next day Georgie wants to show me a video of the twins that had been taken at Small Steps.

The video shows Georgie and Karina – a wonderful physiotherapist who has become Georgie's Girl Friday and lifeline at home – kneeling over Thomas and Alice in the centre of the screen and lifting their arms in the air while singing to them. The twins smile beatifically.

The video flickers and a new scene comes onto the screen.

'Ah, this is what I wanted you to see,' says Georgie.

The twins are now seated on large physio balls, either side of a large table that has been filled with shaving foam. There are three other kids sitting around the table with them. I look at Alice. Her head is twisted back and round to the left and her tongue is darting in and out of her mouth. I realise suddenly that she seems to look very different, here on the screen, from how I'm used to seeing her.

'Watch this,' Georgie says, 'watch Thomas.'

Thomas reaches with his left hand into the foam and makes a determined flick with his hand. The foam splatters up and over the child and carer sitting next to him. His shoulders hunch as he starts to laugh.

'Isn't that great?' Georgie says. Indeed it is great to see Thomas using his hand in a very obviously deliberate manner, but I'm still reeling from seeing the twins on video.

This must be how others see them all the time. On video they look so frighteningly disabled. I must admit I'd never noticed it to that extent before.

I realise that I've been looking at them through rose-tinted spectacles. Every time I'd taken photos of them, I'd always taken ten or a dozen pictures so that one of them might show the twins as I wanted them to be seen, rather than how they actually are. I've been trying to make them look 'normal' all of this time. I guess there's a certain vanity in that, but is that wrong?

And where do we stop with that? In spending hours every day doing exercises that neither they nor we enjoy, are we trying to force our own ways onto them unfairly? How does that make them feel, to be endlessly put through exercises that may never succeed and only make them feel more and more inadequate?

*

The months pass and still there are no discernible benefits from this new treatment.

Georgie and I are carrying out the Scotson therapy on the twins one afternoon as they sleep.

Georgie whispers, 'Thirty seconds doesn't sound very much when you start, does it?'

'True,' I reply.

Our hands go up, down, up down.

'But by the time you've covered every location, three times, and done front and back, done each twin . . .'

'I know,' I chuckle.

'Do you think it's working?' Georgie asks, suddenly serious.

'Um . . . ?' I reply.

'Hmm, me neither,' she says.

Up, down, up, down.

'On to the next miracle cure then?' I say bitterly.

'As it happens, I have just the thing,' Georgie replies. 'It's called hippotherapy.'

'Oh,' I reply. 'Sounds impressive.'

*

It turns out that hippotherapy is just a posh name for horse riding for disabled people.

'There's a place in Surrey called the Diamond Centre,' Georgie says. 'Anthea from Small Steps works there. They do riding for all sorts of disabled people.'

'Really?' I reply. I'm surprised and worried that she might not have thought this through.

'Yes, apparently a centre where we can take the twins.'

'Oh right. How's that going to work?' I ask. The twins' usual seating requires them to be heavily strapped into their seats to hold them in place. They still don't have the ability to sit unsupported.

'I spoke to the Centre; apparently they really can cater for all sorts of people, even those who have such difficulties with balance and tone as the twins.'

'Let's take it for a spin.' I reply.

In for a penny.

*

We arrive at the Centre on the rural outskirts of London one evening soon afterwards – Georgie with the twins in the car and me, straight from work on my bike.

In front of the car park is a large purpose-built barn and we enter into a huge indoor arena. The arena looks like an indoor showground and looking up, there are strips of skylights along the huge canopy of roof.

Three ponies are steadily circling the perimeter of the barn, with riders ranging in competence from those who are just led by the reins to some who are supported by volunteers who walk alongside. Now I see how they do it.

We're greeted by Anthea and the twins beam at her.

'Thomas and Alice have never experienced walking before,' she begins. 'This therapy gives them that experience for the first time; the experience of rolling from side to side as each step is taken and the experience of holding their trunks firm and upright for balance.'

She continues, 'We also believe that the therapy can have a positive impact on other elements of the disabled child's development. We believe that the sensory input that the brain receives from the sensation of riding can support neurological function. We've seen it have a positive effect on physical development, auditory development and even speech and language.'

CURING THE INCURABLE

I have to admit that I'm struggling to see the link between horse riding and brain development, but once again, I recognise the need to leave no stone unturned in our quest to achieve the best for the children. I think back, once again, to the promises I made, whispered through the portholes of their incubators as they lay hanging on to life by a tiny, thin thread.

'Let's get started,' she says.

Riding hats are retrieved for the twins. Even in the smallest hats they can find, they look hilarious. The hats smother their heads – their eyes peek out from beneath the brim and they are smiling at the laughing faces around them, seemingly aware of how ridiculous they look.

Anthea takes Alice first into her arms and then bundles her onto the pony, a chestnut mare called Pepsi who looks stout enough not to be alarmed by an atom bomb.

Pepsi starts to move off slowly around the arena. Anthea stands alongside Alice holding her by her shoulders. Alice's head lolls forward, her chin on her chest. Another helper stands on the other side, supporting Alice's hips and another stands in front, leading Pepsi by a bridle.

As the group moves slowly up one side of the arena, we see Alice's shoulders start to shake.

'Is she OK?' I ask Georgie, concerned that she might be starting to spasm.

'I think she's laughing,' Georgie replies.

Sure enough, as they turn to bring Pepsi back down the hall towards us, there is a huge grin on Alice's face. She has lifted her head from her chest and sits perfectly aligned with Pepsi's head in front of her.

'Oh, wow,' I say.

TWO FOR JOY

It's the first time I have seen her sitting so upright and as she moves towards us I see that only Anthea is supporting Alice now, holding Alice's shoulders lightly with the tips of her fingers. Alice is almost sitting up on her own. Her face is a picture, beaming from ear to ear, as if she knows just how brilliantly she is doing.

'Wow,' I say again.

22. Danse Macabre

Thomas's restlessness is becoming a real concern. It's 4 a.m. and he has been up for much of the night with strong and painful spasms.

Georgie says, 'Can you go, J? It's your turn.'

'What do you mean my turn?' I am insulted. 'I must have gone to him at least six times.'

Nothing, silence.

'Fuck's sake.' I throw the covers back with a pronounced huff and go to him once again, glancing jealously at my wife as she pulls the duvet up over her chin. God that looks nice in there; it's freezing out here.

I try to calm Thomas with my voice, my hands stroking and cajoling him back to sleep.

It's a Saturday morning and later at breakfast we are concerned.

'How many times did you go in the night?' I ask. I can't believe she's been more than me. She was out cold most of the night.

'About nine or ten times.'

'Oh.' I say, deflated. I thought I'd scored more points last night.

'You?' she says.

'About that,' I lie.

'Well, it's a good thing our marriage isn't founded on these conversations we have at night.' She smiles.

'So if we both went that many times, Thomas must have only got half an hour of sleep at any one time,' she continues. 'Let's take him in and see what the doctors make of him. This isn't good for any of us.'

Thomas is lying on a pile of cushions on the floor in the playroom. His body is contorted and jerks in a kind of danse macabre. His back is arched and he's bent backwards in a strange curve. His mouth is wide open and his tongue makes short darting movements. His arms are twisted almost 180 degrees outwards, like an Action Man whose hands have been assembled the wrong way round. His breathing becomes laboured, rasping, and his legs tremble with the force of the spasm. His eyes and nostrils flare like a spooked horse. He seems to be beseeching us to do something to help.

I climb down to him and pick him up, wrestling with his limbs, soothing him with my voice and trying desperately to break the force of the tremor through his legs. It's as if he's possessed by some demonic presence.

Eventually I wrestle him into calm. The spell is broken and his body relaxes. He bursts into tears now that his body has been freed from the grip of the spasms. His legs are twitching like a dying animal's, shivering as the force of the spasm relents.

He lies sobbing in my arms, his eyes intermittently closing

and then he looks up at me again in alarm as he feels the force of another spasm coming upon him like a tsunami.

What hell is this that his body is suffering?

*

It's the middle of the following night and things seem, if anything, to be worsening. Thomas is folded backwards, arching and screaming in pain. He and I have spent the last four hours in the spare bed together and I've now taken him back to Georgie in our bed for her to take over.

I return to the spare room to try to get a few hours. The room looks like an unruly elephant has trampled through it. Tracey Emin's bed wasn't a patch on this. The bed itself is a scene of hillocks and valleys – the sheets shaped like the rugged, papier-mâché landscapes I used to make as a child. The floor is festooned with articles we have attempted to use through the night to calm him: massage oil, toothbrushes to chew on, dummies. And here lie his pyjamas – discarded on the floor as his temperature has risen, the sweat has come and the increasing panic and fear has become so apparent in his eyes.

Later we explain the pattern of events in these recent weeks to the paediatrician.

'We've been up all night with him. I don't think he's had more than half an hour of sleep at any one time. In between times he suffers terrible contortions and screaming. He can't function normally during the day because he's too buckled to sit upright or be held upright. Feeding him is impossible, so he's getting very little nutrition as well.'

The paediatrician looks flummoxed. 'I'm afraid it's not something I've seen before.'

Not the most reassuring words a parent wants to hear: Words, however, that we are going to have to get used to. Our twins will challenge the medical community many times over in the coming years.

'My concern is that this is some sort of neurological condition. Has he had an MRI scan yet?' she asks.

'Yes,' I answer. 'The frontal lobes are fine, in fact the brain itself is fine in all senses, but for the fact that he is missing almost all of his cerebellum.'

At the time we had been told this, it had seemed like this news was something very significant but then, as now, the doctor looked nonplussed. The cerebellum is the large part of the brain at the back, near the spinal column, that assumes responsibility for things like balance. There didn't seem to be an explanation for the fact that Thomas had this large part of his brain missing, other than his difficult start to life. Nor did there seem to be too much concern about it from the doctors: the advice being that Thomas would be able to teach other parts of his brain the skills that the cerebellum would ordinarily handle.

It doesn't seem that it's of particular relevance to this affliction either.

'OK. Well, look. I'm afraid this is a new one on me. I think you need to see a neurologist. Do you have one you see?' she says.

'Yes,' we reply instantly. 'Dr Lin at the Evelina.'

'Perhaps he has the answers,' she says.

'Hope so,' I say.

*

The endless days and sleepless nights continue during the

following week as we wait to see Dr Lin. By the time our names are called in the waiting area, our nerves are frayed, our brains a muddle and Thomas is in constant pain and despair. None of us has slept for days.

Our hopes are high that Dr Lin can provide us with a solution, but our confidence in the medical profession's ability to solve this problem is at a low.

'Let's put you on the floor then, Thomas,' he says.

Georgie lays Thomas on a soft mat on the floor. Immediately he arches into spasm – his mouth is wide open, eyes flashing with panic and discomfort as his head clicks back, his arms swing into straight arcs behind him and his legs push in different directions – the left straight out behind him, toes pointed like a ballerina, the right knee flexed up towards his body.

'Classic,' Dr Lin mutters.

'Excuse me?' I ask.

'Classic, I said. He's a classic case.'

'Of what?' I ask.

'Dystonia.'

'Sorry?' Georgie asks.

'Has no one said the word dystonia to you before?' he asks.

We look at each other, now desperately uncertain that this word might have been included amongst the many medical terms we have been introduced to in recent years.

'Um, no, I don't think so,' Georgie replies.

'OK, well I'll explain in a minute. First of all we need to sort Thomas out. How long has he been like this?'

'Almost two weeks,' I reply.

He tuts beneath his breath then asks, 'Any sleep?'

'No, not for the past ten days, it's been continual,' I reply.

'And you?' he asks.

'No, none for us,' Georgie replies. 'But there are two of us, we take it in turns. It's not the same for Thomas.'

'I'm going to admit him to the ward upstairs.' He turns to the nurse alongside him. 'I'm writing him up for trihexyphenidyl, diazepam and triclofos. The sooner you can get those into him the better.'

Minutes later, the nurse reappears and we hold Thomas as still as possible as the drugs are administered. His teeth clash against the plastic of the syringes as another spasm comes, forcing him to clamp his jaw shut. We hold his mouth open and eventually he swallows the drugs.

The effect is almost instantaneous. Thomas, for the first time in a fortnight, collapses into blissful sleep and stays that way for fourteen hours.

Not long afterwards, we do the same.

As I doze of I think to myself. I like this Dr Lin. What was that word he said again? Dystonia? Yes, that was it. Sounds like a Peter Andre song.

Dystonia . . .

*

It doesn't surprise me at all that dystonia is only one letter away from dystopia. It is a kind of living hell. My laptop hums into life as I log in to *Wikipedia*.

> Dystonia is a neurological movement disorder, in which sustained muscle contractions cause twisting and repetitive movements or abnormal postures. The disorder may be hereditary or caused by other

factors such as birth-related or other physical trauma, infection, poisoning or reaction to pharmaceutical drugs, particularly neuroleptics. Treatment is difficult and has been limited to minimising symptoms of the disorder, since there is no cure available.

No cure again. Bloody marvellous.

After several days Thomas comes home again, apparently and amazingly mended. But by now, Dr Lin has had the opportunity to see Alice as well and she too is diagnosed with dystonia. Her movement disorder is less pronounced than Thomas's, but she also struggles to contain the spasms when they appear. Sitting comfortably is hard for her, her strong extensor pattern means she is often pushing her hips hard against the lap strap in her buggy, which becomes very painful after a short while.

'Clearly medicine is a very effective way of dealing with dystonia, but there are other measures we look at,' says Dr Lin. 'We have recently set up a practice called the complex motor disorders team here at the Evelina.'

Apparently our children have 'complex motor disorders'. Nice.

'Part of our remit is to bring the benefits of deep brain stimulation to kids with dystonia,' he continues.

Deep brain stimulation! Jesus, I thought the word 'complex' was bad.

'We'll give you some literature to take away with you,' he says, 'but briefly, this is a brain implantation where we insert electrodes into the brain which are connected by wires to a battery pack which sits on the chest.'

'You mean brain surgery?'

'Yes. Typically an eight-hour operation.'

'Right.'

'Let me explain how it works.' He continues, sensing the imminent refusal in our bodies and faces. 'Dystonia acts like white noise, bombarding the body with continual neurological charges which make the body's muscles spasm. You've seen the effect that that can have when it rages uncontrollably in Thomas. Alice has the same issue, to a lesser extent, but all the same very much in evidence with her arching and wriggling.

'So the job of the DBS device is to send electrical impulses to interrupt the flood of false information that the brain is sending to the body. This has the effect of stilling the body, reducing the spasms and allowing improvements such as sitting comfortably. This means the child can be fed more easily, taught more easily and so on. It also means things like speech and hand movement can become easier because you haven't got the continual interruption of the irrelevant and distracting white noise coming from the brain.'

It all sounds good. Except the bit about the brain operation. That doesn't sound good at all.

Later in the car, Georgie and I discuss our conversation with Dr Lin.

'No way,' she says. 'There's been enough suffering.'

'Yes, I agree,' I say. 'We're a long way from needing to open up their brains.'

We drive along in silence for a while and then grind to a halt in the late-afternoon London traffic.

'You OK?' Georgie asks.

'Yes,' I say and look across at her. 'I just get a bit maudlin sometimes.'

She looks upset.

'You know,' I continue. 'What might have been?'

She nods and we look at one another.

'It's all my fault,' she says suddenly.

'What do you mean?' I say.

'Life is so hard for you and it's all my fault and there's nothing I can do about any of it,' she replies and her face creases with the beginnings of tears. 'I should have held onto them longer. I've failed you and I've failed them.'

And then she's sobbing and saying through sharp breaths, 'I wouldn't be surprised if you wanted to leave us.'

'That's rubbish, George,' I say. 'Come on, there's nothing either of us could have done.' I reach across and grab her hand. 'It's my fault for dropping Thomas on his head when he was little.'

'No,' she says, looking across at me and we hold one another's eyes for a moment, relieved to have breathed these unspoken fears to one another at last, but still so desperate for it all to be different.

'Come on, George, this is all nonsense,' I say. 'We've just been dealt a shitty hand and we have to deal with it the best we can.

'We're on the up and up now,' I go on. 'We fixed Thomas and they're both making progress. Nothing's going to stop us.'

'I love you,' she says and smiles.

'Me too,' I reply. 'Thank God for you.'

Little do we realise that the events of the past three years are going to look a lot like a teddy bears' picnic in comparison to what will come next. Cerebral palsy will seem a doddle by comparison with the impact of dystonia.

PART 3

DO
DIFFERENT

23. Special Needs

The twins are now four and for all of the difficulties that they have endured they are developing into real characters. Their physical disability becomes more apparent with every passing year, but as they grow, so their intellectual abilities seem to become more evident as well.

Having no speech, communication with the twins is limited to reading their faces for signs of response. We know there is plenty going on in their heads from the way that they respond when someone familiar comes into the room, from the way their faces light up when Georgie or I reach for the cupboard that has the chocolate in it or from how they respond to slapstick humour.

These little signs give us great confidence about the future but all too often we find we are the only ones who can see the planet-sized brains within these mini-Einsteins.

The Maytree Nursery has been great for them so far, they

have made friends and enjoyed the experience of being in a class with other kids, playing and taking part in their activities, but it's clear that their peers are leaving them far behind – however much they seem to love having the twins in their class. And so, as the twins approach school age, we accept, somewhat reluctantly, that some sort of formal specialised setting is going to be needed for them now.

Their time at Small Steps has also been invaluable, the integration of physiotherapy into the school setting has shown us how good a school setting can be, but sadly they are only able to fund a day a week and so we must look elsewhere for a more permanent school.

The twins present an interesting challenge to prospective schools. The main challenge is the difficulty in communicating with them. They can't speak and physically they are, as yet, completely incapable of any kind of independent movement, so using a mouse or sign language is impossible for them. And yet, we know there's plenty going on in there.

The second challenge is their dystonia. Because of the uncontrollable and painful spasms they can't be left in their wheelchairs for long periods of time. So they need to be taken out and handled by expert hands, ideally a physiotherapist, in order to sit comfortably and even be in a position to begin learning.

The third issue is Thomas's questionable hearing. Does the school have experience of dealing with kids who don't hear well? Are they familiar with Makaton and other forms of sign language?

We realise we have a demanding list of requirements and that we are unlikely to be popular with most headteachers with a shopping list like that. Having twins – double the effort and double the cost – just adds to the ask.

It is with this cheery thought in mind that we begin our search for a school for the twins.

I start with a book called *The Good Schools Guide – Special Educational Needs*. It's a beast: 1,085 pages of the best special-needs schools in the country. The length of the book is overwhelming, but I'm also encouraged that the British education system has so much to offer to children like Thomas and Alice.

Every morning on the train to work and every evening on the way home I trawl through the guide, thumbing down the corners of the pages showing those schools that might be suitable – schools which specialise in kids with physical disability. Each school lists the types of disability they specialise in, so where schools are listed as catering for children with moderate to severe CP (I'm still, naively perhaps, hanging on to the idea that their condition might yet turn out to be moderate, despite all signs to the contrary) I mark them down as a possible.

I then draw a map and calculate the distance to all of the schools. I decide to focus my search on schools in the south-east – my job ties me to London, so given the range of choice the book is giving me, I decide not to make life any harder than it needs to be.

Eventually, we're down to fifty-six schools. Plenty of schools to research and very encouraging that there are so many within our reach. I assume, somewhat ignorantly as it transpires, that this means that there is going to be a good range of choice for us.

The next stage of the research involves looking at each of these schools' websites. How many children do they look after? How many with cerebral palsy? How do they bring the best out of them? What's their Ofsted mark like? How do they ensure the safety of the kids? Will the kids be in their wheelchairs all day? What additional activities can they offer?

The search is long and painful, but, I tell myself, not markedly different from the search undertaken by every parent with normal kids.

Eventually, Georgie and I have our shortlist – half a dozen schools across London, Sussex and Hampshire for us to visit. I take a few days off work and our road trip begins.

An inauspicious start at our first school: it has listed itself as a school for children with physical disability, but it's pretty clear that their main focus is on kids with learning difficulties. Also, the school goes up to eighteen. The corridors are filled with hulking teenage giants, whose behaviour seems highly unpredictable. It's very hard to see our tiny, wheelchair-bound kids – still babies in so many ways – finding a home in this environment.

'Yes, I think I know what athetoid cerebral palsy is,' says the headteacher when we meet with her later. Not hugely convincing.

'Do you have any kids with athetoid CP?' asks Georgie.

'Not at the moment,' she admits, in a way that suggests that they may never have had them.

'Are the staff at all familiar with dystonia and how to deal with it?' I ask, more in hope than expectation.

'With what? Sorry?' She replies.

'Dystonia?' I reply.

*

'No,' says Georgie firmly as we make our way to the car park later.

'Agreed,' I reply. First one off the list.

The next day, early in the morning, we visit another school nearby. We have high hopes of this school as it practises conductive education. This is the idea, practised at Small Steps, that you can get the most out of these kids if you integrate physical work with educational learning. The school is great and we sit in on the morning session as the children are prepared to go through their daily routine.

The children are lined up on their floor mats as each is taken through their physio routines by a handler. The handlers sing as they do this and the kids seem to enjoy the experience. All, that is, except one.

Our eyes are drawn to a small blond boy in the corner. He sits apart from the rest of the class in a chair on his own. He is gently rocking his body and shaking his head.

'Bad boy,' he mutters to himself repeatedly under his breath.

None of the teachers or assistants seems to notice him or pay him any attention, so the rocking continues, as does his muttering.

Georgie is clearly rattled by what she has seen in the classroom. There's a very important question we haven't been asking on these school visits and one which can't be asked but one which we know we have to be alert to . . .

'Will you – all of you – love our children without condition?'

*

Three further visits and three further disappointments: The wrong age, the wrong type of setting, not enough character.

In desperation, more than anything, we elect to enrol the twins into our nearest special needs school, in nearby Croydon. The school bills itself as a school for physical disability, but before long, it becomes apparent that they are struggling to know how to deal with our twins. They are used to kids who have greater physical ability, but less cognitive capacity. Georgie spends most of her days at school with the twins during their first term, showing the teachers and assistants how to handle the twins and how to get the best out of them.

I join the occasional session and one morning I'm at the school to help advise their handlers. The teacher has arranged a music session and all of the children in the twins' class are gathered round on chairs in a circle. Alice and Thomas's wheelchairs are brought into the circle and various instruments are handed around from a large plastic box.

The music begins and all of the kids start shaking and banging their instruments. It's an unholy racket. There on the other side of the circle from me, sit Thomas and Alice in their chairs, their instruments – castanets for Thomas and a drum for Alice – sit silent in their laps.

No one has noticed.

*

'I just don't see the point,' says Georgie later when I tell her about what happened. 'It's hopeless.'

'We'll find somewhere,' I say, once again more in hope than expectation.

The reality is that things are closing in on us. Georgie still has absolutely no time to herself, despite the fact that the twins are in so-called full time education.

'Maybe we should just give up,' Georgie says hopelessly. 'Educate the twins ourselves at home. Shut the door, shut out the world and get on with it.'

I know what she means, but I'm also desperate for us all to have some normality in our lives: For the twins to go to school and make friends and learn new things and be inspired by learning. And, just as important, for Georgie to get some semblance of her life back.

The search for a school has been a profoundly isolating experience.

But then luck drops a heap of happy into our laps again.

*

Our friends, Michael and Jane, have enrolled their twins, Marcia and Emerson, at a school in Aylesbury, Buckinghamshire, called PACE. Marcia and Emerson are direct contemporaries of our twins. They were born nineteen days before our twins in the same hospital and we spent a lot of time talking to Michael and Jane during those early months as their twins went along an almost identical trajectory of ups and downs. Their twins have ended up with a similar level of disability as our two.

'It's amazing,' Michael says when we meet for a coffee. 'They use conductive education, they really know what they're doing.'

'How the hell did it slip through my net?' I ask myself, somewhat irritated that my weeks of research might have all been a huge waste of time.

Michael, continues, 'There are about thirty kids, five to eleven, all of whom have movement disorders. The staff are amazing.'

'Sounds great,' I agree. It's good to see Michael so enthusiastic.

'How do you handle the school run?' Like us, they live in South London.

'We're moving,' he replies.

'To Buckinghamshire?' I ask, surprised.

'Yep, house is on the market, we've found somewhere to rent in Amersham.' He smiles. 'Things we do, eh?'

'Wow!' I say, 'You must really love this school.'

*

From the outside, PACE is not much to look at. Hidden away down a short driveway in a housing estate in Aylesbury, it's a single-storey brick building with a covered walkway along the front.

I smile at Georgie as I pull the car up in front of the building.

'Here we go then,' I say, hoping, praying that this might be the answer. I unbuckle my belt as two of the PACE staff approach the car.

'Hi, I'm Heather,' says one, whose face I recognise from the website and whose New Zealand accent I recognise from the phone. 'And this is Josie,' she introduces a young blonde lady. I'm pleased to see that they are wearing the ubiquitous uniform of the physiotherapist – trousers, T-shirts and trainers. Their attire seems to suggest that they're prepared to do some exercise. With our twins, I say to myself, they're going to need to.

I shake Heather's hand as I step out of the car; Josie is already opening up the back door on the passenger's side, reaching in and unbuckling Alice from her seat.

'You must be Alice,' she says. 'C'mon then, let's get you out of there and see how you feel.'

Before I know it, Heather has opened Thomas's door and is taking him out of his seat.

'And you must be Thomas,' she says smiling. 'Your dad's told me a lot about you. Let's get you out and you can show us what you're capable of.'

Georgie and I stand at the side of the car, looking at one another, somewhat surprised. We are so used to people recoiling from the twins or to the twins being overlooked. It's clear that Heather and Josie are far more interested in getting to know our twins by what they tell them with their bodies than what we have to say.

They carry the twins inside and into a large room. It looks more like a gym than a classroom, with all manner of physiotherapy equipment – chairs, physio balls, hoists, standing frames – throughout the room.

Josie says, 'Does Alice have leg gaiters?' After I have retrieved them from the car, she expertly wraps them around Alice's legs. They are long struts, wrapped in padding and Velcro which we put round her legs to provide support when she is standing.

'Let's see you how you get on walking, shall we?' she says.

'Oh, no, she doesn't walk,' I interject, smiling uneasily.

'Oh,' says Josie. 'What do you think, Alice? Would you like to give it a try?'

Alice giggles. I get the feeling my daughter might be about to show me up.

Heather brings a wooden frame around in front of Alice. Josie stands her up and Heather takes her hands and holds them on the frame. Alice stands wobbling, giggling, as Josie props her up from behind.

Then Josie taps her left leg.

'Shall we have a go at lifting this leg, Alice?' she says.

Alice is still giggling and looking at us, thrilled by the new sensation and the disbelieving looks on our faces.

'Concentrate, Alice,' I say, laughing.

Alice slowly lifts her leg.

'Good girl!' Josie encourages her. 'And now down.'

Alice puts her left foot down in front of her right foot.

'That's it,' she says. 'Now the other one.'

Josie holds Alice's left leg firmly, she is bent down so that her shoulder is supporting Alice's bum. Josie is shaking with the exertion of holding this position. She taps Alice's right leg and she lifts it slowly from the floor.

Down it goes again.

She is walking. My daughter is actually walking.

Fuck you, world!

Fuck you, all!

Fuck you, the paediatrician who said this would never happen!

Fuck you, Alice's dad for saying she didn't walk! Yeah! Fuck you!

Oh, hang on, that's me.

*

We've seen and heard enough from this brief visit to know that we have finally found what we have been looking for. We decide to send the twins to PACE as soon as we can and to move house, out to Buckinghamshire.

It's a huge step for us. It will mean that we are far away from our friends and families and it will mean three hours a day of commuting for me, but in a few years filled with difficult decisions this seems like the easiest one we have ever had to make.

Several weeks later, soon after their fifth birthday, the twins enrol at PACE and a month or so later, we make our move out to the countryside.

We have found a beautiful place to rent in a large village near Aylesbury called Haddenham; a sixteenth-century cottage, with its own walled garden and wonderful, spiral brick chimneys rising from its thatched roof. Inside it is all low, beamed ceilings and log fires. We're told by Tony, the landlord, that JFK once spent the night here. It is picture-book perfect for a young family like ours and the ideal country resting point, while we look for a place to buy.

It feels like the sun has finally come out for our family.

24. Mutton

As we settle into our new home and the twins into the routine of their new school, we once again turn our attention to the troubling issue of Thomas's hearing.

The process of getting anyone in authority to take our concerns seriously has been long and desperately annoying.

Finally we succeed in securing an appointment with a specialist audiologist to undertake some analysis and see once and for all whether Thomas is hearing properly. The tests have been done and today is the day when we will be presented with the outcomes.

I arrive late afternoon at the Newcomen Centre at Guy's Hospital, a rabbit warren of buildings and corridors at the back of London Bridge station. Eventually I find my way to the waiting room, where I find Georgie and Thomas. All the tests have been undertaken, and we have been given forewarning of what we might expect, so we have butterflies in the tummy as we wait.

We're the last appointment of the day and are greeted by a young audiologist called Anzel, whom we have been getting to know through our recent appointments. Her serious face as she greets us is an early-warning sign of the message that follows next.

'Come on through,' she says, deadpan, and we dutifully traipse through to the meeting room.

We settle into the room and she begins, 'So, the situation is rather as we expected.'

Disappointment on our faces.

'The tests show that Thomas has a profound bilateral hearing impairment. I'm sorry to say he is deaf in both ears.'

The news we had been expecting, but it still is a heart-sinking moment.

'How come his hearing tests in the neonatal unit were positive?' Georgie asks.

'Hard to say,' replies Anzel. 'Sometimes we find these anomalies. I don't know whether he had hearing and lost it, or the tests were inaccurate.'

'Does it make any difference as far as the treatment is concerned?' I ask.

'Well, not really,' she replies. 'I guess if he's had hearing at some stage, then the chances that he can regain it are better than if he's never had any hearing before.'

Georgie says. 'So what are the next steps? You've previously mentioned a cochlear implant. Is that an option for him?'

'We've discussed it as a team and we do feel that he's appropriate for an implant,' Anzel replies.

'OK, can you tell us more about it?' I ask.

'Sure,' she says. 'The cochlear implant is a device which

comes in two parts – an internal part and an external part. We implant the internal part of the system by making a small incision in the skin behind the ear and placing a device which then connects, via a wire, to the cochlear. Thomas's hearing is prevented because the inner workings of the ear are not functioning properly. So the implant enables us to bypass that area and connect with the cochlear, which then conducts the sound to the brain. . . . With me?' she asks.

We nod and she continues, 'The outer section then sits behind Thomas's ear and will do the job of bringing sound in from the outside world and connecting with the inner part via a magnet.'

'Sounds good,' Georgie says. 'And what expectations should we have for the device once it's up and running?'

'Well, there are three levels of success,' Anzel says. 'The first level is environmental sound and we can guarantee that level is achievable. By that I mean that the implant will give Thomas access to all of the sounds around him. Your voices, music, his sister's chatting, passing cars in the street, for example. So if you hear him crying next door and you're busy, you'll be able to call to him and reassure him that you are nearby.'

'The second level is understanding speech. We don't know whether Thomas will ever be able to achieve understanding, just to warn you. We much prefer to implant kids earlier in life, while the brain's plasticity – its ability to develop other skills from other parts of the damaged brain – remains. There is a chance that the neural pathways that help understanding have closed down after all this time. So we can't make any promises.'

This is a bit of a sore point for Georgie. She has been asking for referrals for Thomas for several years and various events have conspired to delay this diagnosis. The reason he's been diagnosed so late is because of inefficiencies in the system, so it's difficult to hear that the result of these delays could be that Thomas's ability to understand is compromised.

Anzel continues, sensing our disappointment. Bravely she ploughs on, even though she has more bad news to impart.

'The third level is speech for Thomas himself. I can't rule it out altogether, but I have to advise you that the chances of Thomas learning to speak are slim.'

Georgie looks downcast, but I feel strangely calm. The diagnosis feels like a drop in the ocean compared to the twins' cerebral palsy and the ravages of their dystonia. I've just been told my son is deaf as a post and I can't say I'm terribly bothered.

Add it to the list.

25. DBS

And while the picture is getting cloudier in relation to Thomas's hearing, so the troubles with his movement pattern have also been steadily worsening.

The drugs that Dr Lin deployed with such effect on his first admission to hospital a couple of years ago are starting to lose their effect. Initially, we were only administering diazepam to Thomas in emergencies, but we are now keeping him on regular doses of the medication in order to try to keep his dystonic spasms under control. In recent months, visits to Dr Lin and weeks spent on the ward at the Evelina have become much more common.

Thomas moves into our bedroom at night and we take it in turns to sleep for a few fitful hours in the spare room while the other tries to keep him as calm as possible. But it's an almost impossible task – his whole body contorts, his back arches and his limbs twist. And he screams. The screams – each one like a knife. We live in an almost permanent state of fear – terrified by the pain he is suffering and desperate that we seem to be able to do nothing to help him. Our cuddles seem to have almost no effect, but we cuddle him all the same, perhaps for our own benefit more than his. To feel that we are at least trying.

With the increasing deterioration in Thomas's condition and a growing concern about our ability to cope with these violent and protracted spells of dystonia, we decide to return to Dr Lin to discuss the subject of deep brain stimulation (DBS). The medication is no longer proving as useful a barrier against the onslaught as it once did, prompting us to think the once unthinkable: perhaps brain surgery might be the answer after all?

Before the twins can be considered for the surgery they will need to undergo a PET scan to confirm the levels of activity in their brains. Without a reading that shows that normal levels of neural activity are taking place, there is no point in undertaking the DBS surgery.

'Good news,' says Dr Lin as we sit down with him in his office. 'The PET scans show that the twins have the necessary levels of response to proceed with the operation.'

Well, I suppose that is good news, but the unfortunate thing is that this means we are now going to be forced to actually make a decision.

'There are areas of Thomas's brain where we don't see any kind of activity, but that is in his cerebellum, which you remember from the MRI scan is entirely absent, so it is no surprise to not see any activity there,' he says.

'Would that have any kind of bearing on the success of the DBS?' I ask, hoping not to show any excitement in my voice that might betray the fact that I'm grasping at straws – anything that might avoid having to make a decision. 'Have you seen other DBS operations succeed despite an absent cerebellum?'

'No, we haven't seen that, nor do I believe are there published cases of absent cerebellum elsewhere,' he answers. 'However, we have to bear in mind that Alice has a normal cerebellum and also severe dystonia.' He opens his hands, 'I don't think it's relevant.'

'What about the functionality that Thomas already has in his hands?' I ask. 'Also, in his neck and trunk. We often feel that he is using his dystonia to carry out some of these functions. Is the operation going to prevent him from carrying out these functions altogether? In other words, might Thomas actually be left with less function post operation?'

'No, what functions he has he should maintain or improve. That's the objective of the treatment,' he answers calmly. He's been here before: terrified parents, desperate for a way out when the answer is staring them in the face.

I continue with my list of questions. 'Sorry, Dr Lin, I have a long list.'

He smiles, so I continue, 'The twins have just moved to a conductive education setting called PACE in Buckinghamshire. The basis for conductive education is for the children to learn to control their spasms through applying their own physical concentration, and learn to manage their spasms themselves.'

'Yes,' he replies patiently. 'A lot of our kids practise conductive education.'

'OK,' I continue. 'But is DBS really necessary if they can be taught to manage their dystonia for themselves?'

'The reality is, James, that dystonia can't be managed purely by mind-over-matter approaches,' he says. 'You also need to know that the twins won't grow out of their dystonia.'

He seems to sense that this is disappointing news for us and presses on. 'Would you like me to talk you through the process in a little more detail?' he asks.

'OK,' I say, leaning back now.

'As you've heard me say before, Thomas and Alice have secondary, generalised dystonia. This is a more severe type than primary dystonia, which can sometimes just affect one limb or a hand, for example. In their cases, overactive brain impulses bombard the body with irrelevant instructions and this causes their bodies to spasm in the uncontrolled way that you have become used to seeing. Same for their arching, pushing in their chairs and their tongue thrusting.'

'To remind you, the purpose of DBS,' he continues, 'is to knock out those signals. The operation involves implanting electrodes into the brain, which are connected to a battery pack which sits under the skin on their chest. Those electrodes emit signals which are intended to eradicate the storms of disruptive impulses.'

'A bit like a pacemaker in the heart?' I ask.

'If you like,' he replies politely.

Clearly not like a pacemaker at all.

'And what sort of benefits would you expect to see?' I ask, swiftly changing the subject.

'Well, by reducing Thomas's dystonic movements we would hope to reduce his arching when he is seated or prone and to cut down his pushing when he is being carried, or sitting on your knee,' he replies. 'This ought to allow him to stay comfortable in his chairs for longer periods, which will become increasingly important at school. It should make speech easier, it should improve his sleeping and it will mean that he should be less tired and able to concentrate for longer.'

He pauses, then says, 'Simply, it will allow the twins to participate more easily in the world around them.'

Nice, I think to myself. That's exactly what we want.

'How common is it?' I ask.

'There's a long history of DBS use in Parkinson's sufferers, going back as far as 1989. We have been pioneering its use in dystonia and CP sufferers. So far we have done twenty-six operations and we have a long pipeline of others to come.'

'Many like Thomas and Alice?' Georgie asks.

'Fewer than five ex-prems with dystonia have been operated on,' he answers. 'Also, you should know that Thomas and Alice would be the smallest children to have had the operation.'

Georgie breathes in sharply. I have to remember that she feels their pain more acutely than I do.

'Tell us about the process,' I say.

'Well, we are ready to go really. We have done all we need to do in terms of pre-scans and setting a baseline with our physio and OT. We've worked on some expectation and goal-setting and we'll let you have the formal report in a few days.'

'The operation itself takes place at King's College Hospital. We'll admit Thomas the day before and his head will be shaved. To warn you, they are neurosurgeons, not hairdressers, so you'll probably find the odd tuft around the back of his head post op!'

We smile and Dr Lin continues.

'On the day itself, once he has been put to sleep, we will do another MRI scan to map the correct coordinates within

Thomas's brain. The globus pallidus is what we are aiming for and it is a tiny area, only five or six millimetres long, so this targeting exercise is critical.'

'Thomas's head will then be secured in a vice, two horseshoe shaped incisions will be made in the skin on top of his head and the skin will be lifted back. Two holes are then drilled in the skull – here and here.' He points to the locations on the top of Thomas's head.

Thomas smiles at Dr Lin, blissfully ignorant of the conversation's content.

He continues, 'The two electrodes are inserted deep into the brain, one on the left, one on the right side of the brain. "Hubcap" screws are then inserted in the skull to hold the electrodes in place, the skin is folded back into place and secured with staples; probably around fifty staples. The battery pack will then be inserted under the skin on his chest and connected to the electrodes via a thin wire which we run under the skin.'

Georgie's mouth is open.

Dr Lin hurries on, 'Thomas will then spend one or two more nights at King's before being brought back here to the Evelina for ten days' to two weeks' recovery. We'll keep him in a separate room on Savannah Ward in order to avoid infection.'

We sit in silence.

'Listen,' he says eventually. 'I realise this is a big decision but it is a relatively safe procedure. If it was my children, I'd be going through with the surgery, but I've seen the effectiveness of this treatment in lots of other people and I realise that you haven't.'

I don't know what to say. What a decision to have to make.

Finally he says, 'We have a surgery slot available on the

thirtieth of December. Go away and think about it. Give yourselves time to consider the pros and cons . . . As I say, it's a big decision.'

*

We have come down to visit our friends Ben, the oyster guy, and his wife Anoushka, in Cornwall. Ben's company, Wright Brothers, has recently started managing the Duchy of Cornwall's óyster farm down here on the mouth of the picturesque Helford River.

We are on a day trip to St Ives with them and we spend the morning splashing around in the surf with the twins. Ben and I hold the twins and run headfirst into the onrushing waves. We charge time and time again, the squeals of delight from the twins as the waves smash into them are a kind of drug and we go on for what seems like hours at this game. At one point, both Thomas and I are upended by a wave and I momentarily drop him in the water. There's a panic as I scrabble to find him before he sinks to the bottom, but amid all the foam I can't see him anywhere. Suddenly my hands find him and I pull him gasping and giggling out of the surf. Eventually our arms are aching with the exertion and the twins' lips are blue with cold, so we turn back to the beach. The twins burst into tears of protest that the fun is at an end and we laugh to know that they have enjoyed it so much.

After lunch, Ben and Anoushka take the twins off for a walk along the beach to allow Georgie and me some time together to consider our decision. It's a beautiful Cornish afternoon and the sun is warm as we lie down on the sand. Georgie lies next to me and I stroke her hair as we talk.

I think to myself, hasn't Thomas dealt with enough during his short life to have earned the right not to have to deal with such major undertakings? And yet . . .

'I just feel that we have recently entered a phase with Thomas where we really have to ask ourselves whether he is enjoying life,' Georgie says.

'It's true,' I say. 'You give these kids such a wonderful, full life with so many rich and varied experiences, but you're right, in amongst the misery of the dystonic episodes, Thomas has become . . .' I search for the right word, 'kind of withdrawn.'

Georgie puffs her cheeks out and continues, 'He used to be so happy and smiley despite all his difficulties. He used to be so engaging. Now he seems to be losing any kind of connection with the world around him.'

'Hmm,' I reply.

She continues, 'Also, the reality is that we're spending more and more time in hospital. We've had four months of this past year in the Evelina. Think how that must be for him, the suffering he's going through and the displacement.
And when the spasms do come, it's just a kind of living hell. He might as well not be here. The constant pain of those spasms, the total inability to do anything functional . . .'

She trails off, anxious at the inevitable direction the conversation is taking us.

To fill the silence, I say, 'To say nothing of the effect it's having on us.'

'I hardly think that's relevant,' says Georgie immediately.

She can be single-minded about this point. She relegates her own needs to such a deep extent that any suggestion that life has become hard for us, as parents, is a total no-no. And in many ways she's right; if we think life's hard, we don't know the half of how it must be for our twins.

'I guess the point is that life isn't much fun for Tommy at the moment,' she says. 'I know two head operations in the space of six months isn't exactly a picnic, but he just seems to be on a never-ending spiral at the moment.'

She's right, but neither of us can bear the thought of serving as judge and executioner on this decision. We can't bear the thought of adding to Thomas's suffering, even if the outcome does improve things for him.

Eventually she says, 'I think we need to grasp the nettle.'

Georgie rolls over to look up at me. She looks utterly miserable.

'Why us?' she says, her eyes starting to brim with tears.

I gather her in my arms.

She leans into my chest and sobs just one word, over and over.

'Tommy . . .'

26. 'Neurosurgical Theatres This Way'

That's what the sign above the corridor at King's College Hospital says.

NEUROSURGICAL THEATRES THIS WAY

If there was any doubt about what we were doing, the starkness of that sign, of those words, ends it.

Last night, Thomas and I stayed on the ward at King's – me in a camp bed alongside him. I had real trouble sleeping, lying awake through the night, pondering this decision, wondering whether we're doing the right thing. Eventually, I climbed into bed with Thomas, who was sleeping soundly. I put my arms around him and gathered strength from holding him close. My brave, brave boy, who has already endured so much, was about to undertake another major hurdle in his short life.

The swing doors clatter loudly as Thomas's bed is pushed through into the reception area of the operating theatres, and Dr Lin and Richard Selway, the man tasked with the unenviable job of implanting the device into the world's smallest-ever patient, greet us warmly. They're dressed head to toe in gowns and hats and their body language and smiles ooze confidence. All in a day's work.

'Would one of you like to come through to the anaesthetist's room while we put him to sleep?' Richard asks. 'Sorry, we can only have one of you,' he explains.

'George,' I say and she briefly touches my hand before following the bed through to the next room.

The double doors swing shut behind them and clack together three times until they come to a gradual rest.

Shit, I think to myself. This is it then.

*

The operation is due to last eight hours, so we have a long and nervous wait to endure. As the eighth hour approaches, we start to look at our watches with increasing frequency. It becomes a struggle not to glance at the clock every few seconds. We chat about meaningless things to occupy the time – anything to distract us from the only thing that means anything to us at the moment – but soon the conversation dries up.

Eight and a half, nine hours . . . is everything OK?

After ten hours, we hassle the ward nurses and ask if they can provide us with an update. They call down to the operating theatre.

'He's just come out,' the nurse explains as she hangs up the phone. 'He's in the recovery bay. You can go down to him in ten minutes. They'll call up when they're ready.'

We're temporarily reassured, but won't feel completely at ease until we see him.

Eventually the ward phone rings again and we are on our way downstairs.

In the corner of the recovery suite, Thomas is stirring. He wears a large turban-style bandage on his head and his face looks bloated, his eyes puffy. He is just waking and starting to wonder what's going on. As soon as he sees us his body stiffens, he starts crying and then screaming.

Georgie runs across to his bed and envelops him in a hug, smothering him in kisses. Her quiet words into his neck start to calm him. His crying stops, subsides to sobbing and eventually his body relaxes into her arms. His misery is difficult for us to take, but it's also immediately reassuring that he still recognises us.

Richard Selway and Dr Lin appear at the bedside.

'How did everything go?' I ask urgently, conscious that this operation will have been something new for Richard, as well as us, given Thomas's tiny size.

'All good,' he smiles reassuringly. 'No issues, complications. He did really well.'

'And you got everything where you needed to get it?' I ask.

'Absolutely,' he assures.

*

The next evening, on New Year's Eve, Thomas is transferred back to the Evelina and into a cubicle at the back of Savannah Ward.

From the window, there is a narrow gap between the buildings on the river front, and, for the second time in five years, I watch the spectacular New Year fireworks across the river. The bright flashes light up our small room, the colours dancing on Thomas's sheets and his turban.

The loud bangs won't wake him, he is still deaf as a post, but I think ahead to his next big operation – the cochlear implant – and look forward to the day when I might call his name and he might hear me.

'Here's to you, Tommy,' I say raising a warm celebratory can of beer I've managed to smuggle into the room. 'You utterly fantastic, hard bastard.'

*

The following week, my dad comes bustling into Thomas's cubicle, all smiles and laughs and huge, all-enveloping hugs. The plastic bag he's carrying clinks as he wraps his arms around me – the unmistakable sound of wine bottle on wine glasses.

The nurse raises her eyebrows . . . 'I'll pretend I didn't hear that!' She smiles.

We giggle like bashful schoolboys.

'Like the beard,' says Dad.

'Ah thanks . . . Haha! It's not a fashion statement. Tommy and I are having a facial-cranial race to see who can grow their hair fastest. He's bald as a coot underneath all that bandaging.'

'You look just like your grandfather,' says Dad. It takes a second before I realise he's talking about me, rather than Thomas.

'Well, I'm hoping I can channel some of Groni's bravery with the beard,' I reply. Groni had commanded a Second World War submarine at the age of just twenty-two and then become a spy behind the Iron Curtain during the Cold War. He had been responsible for some ridiculously brave undertakings at a very young age.

'I'd love to hear more about Groni's early days, Dad,' I say once he has checked on Thomas's progress. I knew my grandfather only when I was a small boy and teenager. Tragically, he hanged himself while I was at university – the pressures of his early days had eaten away at him throughout his life and finally caught up with him in his later years.

'Well, you know the story about Corfu harbour, don't you?' says Dad, relaxing into a lurid orange, plastic armchair. Thomas has fallen asleep now.

'Tell me again.' I'm eager to hear it again – to fortify myself with the fact that my forebear dealt with – and defeated – far more problematic situations than the one that faces me now.

He begins to tell the story of how HMS *Torbay* – the most decorated submarine in the British Navy – blew up half of Corfu harbour and my grandfather earned the Distinguished Service Cross in the process.

'Well, it was Groni's first patrol, 1942 I think it was, and he was Navigating Officer. Corfu harbour was being used by the Axis navy as a key supply site for crossing the Mediterranean to Rommel's armies in North Africa. So it had assumed significant strategic importance and the harbour had been secured with almost impenetrable defences.'

It feels good to be talking about something other than medical procedures.

'The harbour is shaped like a U, with an island set in the middle,' he says. 'At one entrance, there was a narrow channel guarded by a submarine net, which was only lowered when shipping passed into the harbour. At the other end, they had laid a minefield below the surface to prevent submarines from entering. For some reason, Groni, and his commanding officer, Crap Miers . . .'

'Is that the one whose interview technique involved punching Groni in the face to see how he'd react to pressure?' I ask.

'Ha-ha! That's the one,' replies Dad. 'Yes, he had some, er, controversial techniques but having a go at Corfu harbour probably ranks as his most insane effort.'

I smile, and then Dad continues, 'Well, these two lunatics seemed to agree that Corfu harbour could be breached. So they waited all day for the right moment and as merchant ships passed into the harbour, they guided the submarine directly beneath a ship as the net was lowered. Something of a tight fit, but they made it through safely.'

'Unfortunately, waiting underwater to choose the right moment to come into the harbour had drained the submarine of its battery life and they needed to be at full power if they were going to make an assault on the harbour and beat a speedy retreat,' he continues. 'So they waited for night to fall and after dark they took the submarine up to the surface so they could recharge its batteries.'

Thomas's sats monitor suddenly sounds as his oxygen level drops. I reach across to silence the alarm and watch as his oxygen level picks up. The sound is a little like the ping of a submarine's sonar and my heart still lurches when I hear it, just as Groni's must have through the decades of nightmares after he left the Navy.

'It was a bright, moonlit night,' Dad continues, 'and they must have been terrified as they sat on the surface, in full view of the warships anchored in the harbour, as they waited, a sitting target, for the batteries to top up. Talk about going into the wolf's lair.'

Dad is warming to his role as storyteller now, so I draw the cork on the bottle of Rioja he has brought with him. *Clop!* goes the cork, momentarily stopping Dad in his tracks as we sit, giggling, sshhing and hoping that no one has heard.

We pause, listening for footsteps outside.

All well, and I pour the wine into the glasses.

'The wine's great, Dad, but you really didn't need to worry about the glasses.' I say.

'Have to do things properly, Jass,' he says, and I have to admit that I'm glad to be holding a nice warming glass of red wine in my hand, rather than a hospital mug or plastic cup. It's a small slice of normality in this still alien environment.

He continues . . .

'At dawn, *Torbay* was ready, the torpedoes were loaded and they ran the submarine close to the ships in the harbour and opened up, sinking two huge supply ships in the process.'

'For seventeen hours they were chased around the harbour by the destroyers and more than forty depth charges were dropped from a plane above. Eventually, they realised they would have to bite the bullet and make their escape.'

'But how?' he asks rhetorically.

'Through the minefield, obviously!'

I laugh, enjoying the story again and relishing the tales of never-to-be-repeated derring-do from a bygone era.

'So they turn the submarine towards the exit and go hell-for-leather towards the minefield, with the depth charges dropping down around them from the Italian boats up on the surface. As the minefield approaches, they drop the speed down to a crawl as they begin the long and nerve-racking tiptoe through the minefield.

'Dad told me they could hear the mines scraping down the side of *Torbay*'s hull as they crept through the minefield. Meanwhile, all hell was still breaking loose up on the surface, boats zipping this way and that and depth charges being dropped around the submarine.'

'But, as you know, they made it,' he says, finishing the story.

'It's not surprising he ended up so screwed up after facing situations like that,' I say sadly. I know that my father was hit badly by his father's suicide.

'Funny how much the beard makes you look like him,' says Dad, swirling the wine thoughtfully in front of him.

'Well, with any luck I can channel some of that bravery,' I repeat. 'It's a reminder to me that however tough this situation gets, at least I'm not at the bottom of a murky ocean with the pressure of having my crew's lives depend on the decisions I make.'

'Hm,' says Dad. 'In many ways, that's exactly where you are, my boy.'

'Ha-ha! In some ways, maybe you're right,' I reply.

We clink glasses.

27. Tommy Titanium

Thomas's recovery following the brain surgery is longer and bumpier than we expected and in the end he spends another three weeks in hospital before he is deemed well enough to bring home. His movement disorder remains highly erratic and unpredictable and even after several months, it's hard to see that the DBS has had any discernible benefit. However, time is ticking for the cochlear implant and so, come the summer, we are back at St Thomas' for his second major head operation.

Anzel patiently steps us through the process one more time, the day before the surgery.

'It's a much quicker process than the DBS, you'll be pleased to hear,' she begins. 'It usually takes a couple of hours. We need to shave the head around the site behind the right ear and then an incision is made behind the ear and a small hole is drilled through the skull into the middle ear and the cochlear itself.

They will then make a hole in the skull to house the magnet that sits beneath the skin. The device is inserted and then the skin sewn up.'

Piece of piss.

'There'll be some testing done in theatre,' she continues. 'So it might take a little longer with Tommy as we need to ensure that the electrical signals from the cochlear and the DBS aren't interfering. Dr Lin is going to attend the surgery to ensure that all the tests are done accurately.'

Once again, Tommy is proving to be something of a guinea pig. It is highly unusual to have two implants in the head and it has been impressive to see the coordination between the audiology department and the neurology department as they calculate how best to make the two devices work alongside one another. Dr Lin loves a new challenge and we have once again benefited from his boyish enthusiasm.

'Post-surgery, we wait for a few weeks to make sure that the device has taken before we switch it on,' she continues.

'Won't it be a huge shock for Tommy?' Georgie asks. 'His dystonia is very sensitive to any environmental change.'

'Don't worry,' calms Anzel. 'We start very quietly and turn the volume up very gradually.'

'Let's do it,' I say, and before I know it we are once again wheeling Thomas into the anaesthetists' antechamber. I take him out of his bed and sit with him on my lap as the anaesthetist closes in and places the mask over his face. He bursts into tears in protest, his body bucks and head swings from side to side as he desperately tries to free himself from the mask.

Poor blighter, I think, he knows only too well what this means. He has been here so many times before, probably a dozen operations in his short life already. The only thing he doesn't know is how he's going to feel when he wakes up. Will it have been a short operation – last year he had his kidney stones lasered, for example – or will it be something major, like a brain operation, where he wakes up with a stinking headache and it takes weeks to recover? There has been no way to communicate any of this to him.

'Sorry, Tommy,' I say as his fighting finally relents and his body relaxes as the drugs take hold. 'It's another big one.'

*

Thomas has a new nickname: Tommy Titanium. Partly on account of how bullet-proof he seems to be, partly because of the amount of metal he now has in his head.

We have been given a special X-ray scan of his head along with an explanatory medical letter that we have to take with us if ever we need to take him through airport scanners. He reminds me of a very small Robocop.

*

Several days after the operation Thomas comes home, but once again the recovery is prolonged and worrying, requiring an ambulance dash back to hospital on one occasion when he appears to have a fit.

He recovers eventually and a few weeks later we find ourselves back at the audiology department with Anzel for the cochlear implant to be switched on.

We are ushered into a soundproofed room. Our voices sound dead in here, muffled by the absence of any acoustics.

Anzel takes out a small device that looks like a hearing aid

– a small piece of plastic that she fits behind his ear. Attached to it, via a thin, short piece of wire, is a small magnetic disc, which she places on the patch of skin behind Thomas's right ear, where the hair is still growing back following the surgery.

She urges us to be quiet and then fiddles with the laptop in front of her, which is connected to Thomas's new listening device.

She calls his name, softly at first, and then gradually more loudly.

Thomas is having a floppy day, a day where he is super relaxed, and his chin is resting on his chest. On the days where his dystonia is not taking hold, this is the default setting for him, increasingly so as he has started to disappear into himself, owing to his inability to engage with the world around him.

'Tommy,' Anzel calls again. It's clear she is developing something of a soft spot for Thomas.

'Tommy!' A little louder again.

Suddenly he lifts his head and looks in her direction, smiling.

'Good boy, Tommy!' she exclaims and there is already a tear in the corner of her eye.

28. Home Sweet Hospital

A few months later and it's Alice's turn for DBS.

The hardest reaction we face from friends and family when we tell them we're going ahead is, 'Oh right, so you've seen improvements in Thomas since the operation then?' The answer is well, not really, but we can't deny that we have seen it work over short periods.

We also can't ignore the truth that is growing before our eyes every day. Alice is getting bigger and her spasms are getting stronger. Not only are we struggling to cope with the force of these movements now, but it's also evident that Alice is increasingly finding these spasms painful, distressing and, as Georgie points out, humiliating.

We are at the final, pre-operative assessment with all of Dr Lin's team – her operation is a month away. She has scored the lowest possible score on her physical assessments and their advice is pretty conclusive: she needs DBS.

At the same time, they are very pragmatic about the likely outcomes for Alice from the surgery and I can't help feeling disappointed by their predictions.

Kylee, the team's physiotherapist, explains, 'We feel that DBS is likely to improve the prospect of eye gazing becoming a possibility for Alice.'

We have heard this before from other physios and it has always been disappointing news. When a child can't speak or use their hands or feet to control a mouse, the last resort is eye-pointing. This is the process by which a child indicates choice by using their eyes. For example, you might hold a banana and an apple up and ask them which they would prefer and they would make their selection by pointing with their eyes. It's about as rudimentary a form of communication as one can imagine and doesn't seem to have much in the way of potential.

With this viewpoint, I will discover that I am, once again, very wrong.

'I think it would be a mistake to promise that Alice will gain sufficient skill to be able to operate a switch successfully,' Kylee continues. Switches are large plastic discs which are connected to a PC or other device that just need to be touched in order to make a choice. 'But, who knows, that might be added later.'

'We were working under the assumption that eye gazing would be possible for Alice, even without DBS,' I say, failing to hide my disappointment. Georgie reaches across and holds my hand to still the frustration in my voice.

Hortensia, the team's occupational therapist, says, 'The times when you challenge Alice are the times when you tend to see her succeed, but she is still inconsistent. The DBS ought to help to reduce the fluctuations.'

Our hope is that the treatment will also assist with Alice's speech. In recent months, she has started to use her voice much more, thanks in large part to the confidence she is gaining at her new school. The words are approximation, but identifiable words nonetheless. She calls Tommy 'Tinker' and her 'Daddy' is also increasingly easily identifiable.

All in all, we feel that the surgery will improve her quality of life and make day-to-day living more straightforward for her.

*

That night, by the time I've finished clearing up downstairs, Georgie is already in the bath. She looks so lovely lying there in the warm bath, surrounded by snow-white bubbles. I'd say she is the picture of relaxation and contentment, but for the fact that she's tapping away intently on her iPhone.

The urge to join her is too strong and I strip and climb into the bath behind her.

'Budge up,' I say as I climb in.

'J!' she protests and shuffles up the bath, her fingers still tapping away on the device. 'I've got to do my emails . . .'

'Seriously?' I complain. 'Now? Who to?'

'School, wheelchair service, Local Authority,' she says, still typing. 'We need to find eighteen grand from somewhere to pay for Alice's eye gaze computer, two grand for each of their bikes and then another grand for each of their second-skin suits. I just can't see how we're supposed to make it all add up.'

But I know how I can get her to unwind. She needs to stop thinking about the twins for one second and just relax.

I soap my hands and then start massaging her back and her shoulders.

'Come on,' I say, 'put that thing down.'

'No, J,' she says, 'it's important, I don't have any time during the day to send these.'

I continue massaging her back, moving up to her neck now, but she pulls away from me.

Is emailing really more important than a few minutes of relaxation in the bath? I think to myself. So I lean back while she types away and self-pityingly wish that we lived in a world where things weren't so different from the lives we imagine that everyone else has.

*

The date for Alice's surgery is set for 6 October and before we know it, it has arrived.

Georgie and I agree that it's almost worse now that we know what to expect. For me, it feels more difficult because it's my little girl. By the day before the operation I feel like bursting into tears every five minutes.

The morning comes and the porter arrives to wheel Alice down to the operating theatre. She giggles furiously as we trundle along the corridors and Georgie and I struggle to contain our tears and smile back. We have spoken to Alice about the impending surgery but it's hard to know how much has sunk in.

Georgie takes Alice into the theatre and I pace the corridor outside, gurning and grimacing, everything and anything except crying. Having just signed yet another consent form which says that we understand that a stroke or death is a possible outcome of the surgery, it's hard to drive bad thoughts out of my head.

Will I see her alive again? Will I see her smile again? Why the fuck do we have to put her through this?

*

Needless to say, the operation goes smoothly.

'Textbook, would you say?' I ask Dr Lin in recovery.

'If a textbook had been written yet then yes, that operation would have been in it,' he says.

After the problems we had post op with Thomas, Alice's first twenty-four hours feel like a picnic. She sleeps intermittently, but because they and we have learnt to manage the pain more proactively, she seems more comfortable than her brother was and is soon smiling. After several days in the hospital, things are beginning to look a little more promising and so my outlook improves. The half-empty glass now looks a little fuller and life feels more controlled again.

After all, I think to myself, how many fathers get to lie in bed with their daughters on a weekday morning playing fart tennis?

'Stinky Daddy!' she exclaims and we burst into fits of giggles: Alice because she has a tawdry sense of humour; me because it's the first time I've heard her put two words together.

*

Two beds along from Alice, a child has died this morning.

The curtain is drawn around that bed space. The team all wear the same mournful, respectful faces. We parents – the same.

The noisy undercurrent of the ward's bings and bleeps is punctuated with the sound of the child's mother wailing in agony. The sound of her sadness starts soft and then grows in an uncontrollable tidal wave of misery. It's a visceral and unnatural sound; every cry stabbing my heart like a knife.

The fear rises in the back of my throat, the realisation of the fragility of life despite all of these wonderful people and their knowledge. Guilt too, that my children fight on while another has lost its life.

And finally relief that this is an experience that we haven't yet gone through, despite coming so close on so many occasions.

Our twins battle on.

*

After three days boxed up in the hospital, the opportunity to get outside is a welcome one. The hospital smells permeate your body and become your smells. The air, which tastes heavy with the sick, fills your lungs. I walk taller through reception as I see the sun shining and the sky bright blue with the promise of morning. I step out into the cool air eagerly anticipating my first breath of pure air for days. I step out of the door, the sunshine hits my face and I inhale deeply.

Eurgh! Christ!

The stinky sting of exhaled cigarette smoke hits the back of my throat.

Next to me a man whose sickly skin colour defies categorisation sits wheelchair-bound in his grey-green pyjamas with a drip hanging from his arm. He sucks on his cigarette like it's his last, which, from the looks of him, it might well be. Ah, the unholy fixture of every NHS hospital, the ever-incongruous smokers' shelter.

Let's have another go at sucking up that nice clean breath of fresh air after a few more paces, shall we?

*

It's now autumn. Nine months since Thomas's DBS surgery and three since Alice's. It's been wonderful to see Thomas start to hear for the first time, but I'd be lying if I said that we are seeing any kind of physical improvements from the DBS.

Georgie and I begin to wonder whether the surgery has been worth it. Thomas's dystonic episodes continue and Alice's nights are still very disturbed. Georgie and I are up half a dozen times each most night. Truth be told, it seems that the process of determining the right settings for their DBS electrodes is something of a game of hit and miss.

Thomas's settings have been changed several times already. Dr Lin assures us that it's a question of time, but after another particularly nasty episode we decide to return to hospital to see whether another alteration to the settings might have a positive effect.

Georgie, Thomas and I drive down to London, to the Evelina. By the time we reach the hospital, both of them are in tears – Thomas from the exertions of his muscle contractions, Georgie's from tiredness and frustration because she can't make him comfortable. We catch the lift to Savannah Ward on the fourth floor, where I take Thomas out of his chair and hold him to try to ease his discomfort. He arches again, a huge movement, from top to toe and his face once again contorts with the effort and the pain of it. The spasm eventually subsides after a minute and as it recedes he looks up and smiles, as if to reassure me. Sometimes he lives up to the bravery of his namesake in a very obvious way.

Dr Lin arrives with his laptop. 'Right!' he says, resolutely. 'Tell me.'

'Well,' says Georgie. 'It's that left leg again which seems to be triggering things. It goes into spasm, locks up and then the head goes back and the arms twist and he's off.'

'OK, so we need to address the left-hand side then,' replies Dr Lin.

Thomas is on my lap, but unable to sit normally. He lies across my lap as stiff as a surfboard, his head wrenched to the side and eyes flashing in panic. It's an all too familiar sight. His throat constricts with the effort and he makes a rasping sound.

Dr Lin taps on his laptop and then brings the connecting device up to the processor which sits beneath the skin on Thomas's chest.

'I'm going to change the voltage on the right-hand side to see whether we can improve things. The higher right-sided electrodes are implanted into part of the globus pallidus that correlates to Thomas's lower body on the left-hand side . . .'

He taps again and looks up from the screen to see if the change has had any effect.

Almost instantaneously, Thomas relaxes. His tremoring leg eases and the rest of his body flops forward. I gather him up into a more comfortable seating position and he emits a long, relieved sigh.

He takes several deep breaths and then smiles.

'Wow!' Georgie and I say in unison. 'That's incredible.' We look at each other.

OK, *now* we get it.

29. Home

Since we moved to Buckinghamshire we have been trying to find a house to buy. A place which is more in keeping with the needs of our family and a place which we can start to call home.

For the past two years, our Haddenham cottage has been home and we love it, but we want to buy and we have to recognise that the low ceilings, narrow corridors and crumbling walls are not well suited to our needs.

We search for several months before the ideal house suddenly lands in our lap. It has been on the market for some time, but the owners have recently dropped the price so that it comes into the very top of our range for the first time.

The house is in a remote village, a small collection of houses around an eighteenth-century stately home. We know the area a little and have always been fond of its rolling hills and lovely views. The house itself is large, square and modern, perfect for our needs, with the right number of bedrooms and even a separate flat above the garage. We need more and more help with the twins and are reluctantly realising that we will soon need to have a live-in carer to help with the twins' mornings and night times. The house will allow for that.

The twins have their own bedrooms and the downstairs is large and open-plan – ideal for navigating with their wheelchairs – and there are no steps through the house. Importantly, there isn't a room in the house where I can't stand up straight – a nice change from our previous home. Outside, the garden is large but simple. Low maintenance, I think to myself. Perfect again.

Within weeks of arriving here, the family is extended by one as the twins' new carer, Kelly, moves into the flat above the garage. She's a twenty-three-year-old lass from Preston, with a broad Lancastrian accent, a shock of pink hair and a tongue stud. Little do we know, at this stage, just what a wonderful addition she is going to make to our family.

Things are coming up roses.

30. Alone

Sometimes it feels to me as if the issue isn't how we're adapting to life with the twins; it's about how difficult so many other people seem to find it.

It's a trite thing to say, but you learn who your real friends are in these situations. It's a salutary lesson seeing our friends' and siblings' circles of friends expand after the arrival of their children – our godchildren, our nephews and nieces. Their social circles seem to grow ever larger and they are constantly talking about new friends whom we have never heard of before. It's a struggle to keep up.

'Are their kids at nursery with yours?' we will ask.

'No, we met them through NCT,' they'll say. 'Come on, we told you about them when we saw you last time! So-and-so is Such-and-such's godmother! You met them at the christening.'

Partly, I realise bitterly, it's because we don't really want to remember. We never had NCT classes and we don't get the opportunity to meet other parents at the school gates.

The honest truth is that while the birth of their children has expanded the social circuit for our friends and siblings, for us it's done the opposite.

We quickly drift from friends who find it uncomfortable to be with the twins – anyone who struggles to be natural with them. Friends stumble over their sentences with us – the dread in their eyes as they struggle for the right word – 'disabled', 'retarded', 'handicapped', 'spastic' – what's OK? What's not OK? They've not had to deal with this perplexing set of rules before and now it's confronting them at close quarters, with their close friends, and the discomfort is evident. I don't blame them. I was frightened once too.

Georgie tells me about a conversation that she has had recently with a friend. They had been talking about the hard work involved in being a parent.

'Just think,' the friend had said, 'in ten or twelve years all of this is going to be over, the kids will have finished school and left home and we can all start to look forward to our retirements, to holidays away as a couple and living without these constant responsibilities.'

And then there are the friends for whom it comes naturally. They're down on the floor with the twins, playing with them, smothering them with kisses, and for these people, the rewards are instant, hugely gratifying and can often bring a tear to the eye. My admiration for their enthusiasm, their unconditional love and total absence of fear is enormous.

As for meeting and making new friends, the opportunities are few and far between. Most people are too afraid to invite the twins to birthday parties and the like. I'm sure they think about it, but then maybe it seems like it might be too much hard work, too much of a distraction, too uncomfortable for the other guests, so they think better of it.

And you can understand their reticence. I sometimes catch myself looking at the twins and thinking – 'only a parent could truly love that'. Their bodies contorted with spasms, groaning in pain and incapable of communicating in any understandable way.

And then there are the starers. You see them coming as you walk along the pavement.

About ten metres out you see them notice the wheelchair. Then they look at the child and take in their faces. At about five metres out they're trying to work out what's wrong, so now they're really concentrating, really staring. With about two metres to go, their brains suddenly realise they're staring and that there's something wrong and this is the point they normally look up to the person pushing the chair.

Kelly has a great line. She looks the starer in the eye and says, 'Hello, this is Alice. She'd love it if you talked to her. Do you want to say hello?'

Their faces whip away, flustered, as we pass, but I wish they would stop and say hello. I can't help feeling they might learn something important.

To stop bringing the twins out in public would prevent them from enjoying so many pleasures and privileges that we all take for granted.

All of which adds to the sense of increasing loneliness. We are happiest when we shut the door to the outside world and exist just as a family.

At night I tuck the twins into bed. As I have done every night that I've been there at bed time I tell them that I love them. As

I tuck Alice in, she lifts her head from the pillow, focusing hard on trying to return the words to me, but after several seconds, her head falls back and she smiles instead.

'I know,' I say, 'I know you do.' And I kiss her goodnight.

*

'How are you, mate?'

My best friend, Anthony, and I are sitting on towels on the beach at Wells-next-the-Sea in Norfolk. We have come away on our summer holidays with our twins, Anthony and his family and Romayne, Georgie's best friend, and her family.

'Good, mate,' I reply, noncommittally.

'That's not what I mean,' he laughs. 'How *are* you?' he asks again.

'Oh, that,' I say.

Georgie has taken the twins down to the water's edge with Kelly. Ant's boys are proving quite a handful for his wife, Nat, who is attempting to hold their interest with sandcastles.

'Yes, not bad,' I say.

Suddenly Oliver, Ant's four-year-old runs off from the sandcastle and along the beach. At the same time, Toby, their two-year-old races off in the opposite direction.

'Pretty good, all told . . .' I continue.

'Ant!' shouts Nat.

'Shit,' he says and jumps up, sprinting off in the direction that Oliver has just run off in. The beach is crammed with holiday makers and it doesn't take long for kids to disappear altogether.

I look down to the sea front where my own family are sitting in the surf. Georgie and Kelly are sitting with the twins in front of them, kicking the twins' legs and splashing each other to the twins' delight. Their distant screams and giggles reach me up the beach.

Five minutes later, Ant returns with Oliver. He looks stressed.

'Christ, sorry about that,' he says. 'He completely vanished.'

'You want to get yourself a couple of nice disabled kids, mate,' I say, pointing down to the twins at the water's edge. 'Much less stressful.'

Ant laughs at the joke and settles down on the towel again, with Oliver on his lap.

'You were asking how I was,' I say.

'Hm?' he replies. 'Oh yes, sorry, tell me.'

'Pretty good, all told,' I say. 'We're making peace with this situation.'

'That's fantastic, mate,' he replies.

I continue, 'I think we're doing well, I think we're coping well as parents and doing the best we can to make sure Thomas and Alice have everything they need.'

'Good for you, J,' he says.

'But . . .' I pause.

'Yes?'

'Oh, I don't know. I just feel like sometimes we are going through the motions,' I confess. 'We're so busy being carers to these children, so involved in every medical, physical aspect of their care that we never get our heads up out of the sand and think like parents. I just get the sense that life is happening to them, rather than the other way around.'

I pause to make sure he's following me. Christ, why have I become so bloody earnest all the time. I used to be fun!

But I continue with the theme, 'What might *they* like to do?

How can we expand their horizons? How can we bring new experiences to them?'

I pause, then say, 'When they were babies in intensive care, I used to make so many promises to them about what their lives were going to be like: holidays abroad, the best school, fun playing sports together . . . but I just haven't been able to deliver on any of those promises because they're so . . . disabled.'

'Because they're so disabled?' he interjects. 'Or because you haven't thought more carefully about how you can make that happen?'

I look at him, slightly affronted that for the first time, someone is brave enough to question the way I've been going about things. Most people are too afraid to offer an opinion, for fear of causing offence. Most people feel unqualified to pass comment. Not Anthony, he's nothing if not frank.

'You might want to think about what you *can* do,' he says eventually. 'This is their childhood rushing past, a time when they are happiest. Days like this provide the memories that will sustain them when they're fully grown.'

He pauses while we look out at the kids, then he says, 'Remember the holidays we used to have together when you and I were young?'

'Of course,' I say. 'Happy days.'

'Exactly,' he says.

'I should,' I say. 'I really should. Otherwise life's just rushing past . . .'

Two weeks later, I make a new discovery and the bar gets raised.

Really quite high.

31. Keep on Running

I'm sitting at work one morning when a friend sends me an email with a YouTube link.

The short video tells the story of Rick and Dick Hoyt, a father and his disabled son from the US. Dick's gravelly American accent provides the voice over:

> January tenth, 1962. We knew there was something wrong, but we did not know exactly what. The doctor said, 'Forget Rick, put him away, put him in an institution, he's going to be nothing but a vegetable for the rest of his life.'

However, behind his physical disability, they noticed his responsiveness – his eyes were alive. They strongly believed that he could lead a fulfilling life.

They were right. They have built a voice system which allows

Rick to speak, he has gone through school and even graduated. He is a huge sports fan.

And then the bit that really hits home . . . Dick runs marathons with Rick in his wheelchair.

Rick says that when he runs with his father, he feels like he is actually competing with everyone else. They also compete in triathlons together. Dick pulls Rick in a rubber dinghy during the swimming, he cycles with a specially adapted bike with Rick on the front and then he runs pushing Rick in his wheelchair.

The film ends with Dick saying, 'You can do it. You can do anything you want to, as long as you make up your mind, you can do it.'

As it ends I realise I have a lump in my throat and a tear in my eye. I hope no one at work has noticed!

Wow. What an inspirational story. Not just Dick's realisation that Rick was capable of so much more than the doctors thought, but also what Rick has achieved with his life after such inauspicious beginnings: joking to his family through his voice machine, playing hockey in the street with his brothers and then going off to university on his own and graduating.

This last point in particular is an epiphany for me. I'd assumed that the twins would always live with us, even as adults. It had never occurred to me that they might not actually want to live with us when they grow up.

I'm starting to see my children as individuals for the first time. They are going to grow up with their own desires and dreams, whatever their disabilities, and they are going to want their space and freedom. I'm at once excited and terrified by the prospect.

And of course, the inevitable thought that what Dick does as a father, I should also be doing. I slowly realise that my efforts with my children are coming up a bit short. I need to think more about what it's like for Thomas and Alice. Despite their disabilities they are striving to succeed with their limited abilities every day. Yes it takes massive efforts of will for Alice to speak a word or for Thomas to put a piece of cheese in his mouth, but they do it through force of will.

Rick and Dick's story makes me realise that I haven't really been trying. Dick has become the personal embodiment of his son's struggles.

I've been so focused on the day-to-day survival looking after these kids that I haven't really thought properly about how to achieve the unexpected with them. I'd like to take them to the top of a mountain, but we can't. I'd love them to experience the feeling of wind on their faces as they rush down a ski slope, but it'll never happen. I desperately want to play football and cricket with my twins, but I can't do it. I think back to the fathers in the park playing football with their kids – the misery and loneliness of that moment.

Dick and Rick tell me that anything's possible.

Since the experience of that third night after Thomas's birth, he has been something of a hero for me – someone I look to for inspiration in difficult times. Thomas made a conscious decision to survive that night, spurred on, I have to believe, by my whispered promises to him.

I suddenly realise that I just haven't been trying hard enough.

*

Which is how, on a blistering hot June day, several months

later, Thomas and I find ourselves lining up with 1,000 other runners in our local 10-kilometre race in Thame, Oxfordshire. Thomas is in his wheelchair and I'm in my trainers.

The organisers have taken some convincing to let us participate. There are obviously health and safety concerns with having a metal wheelchair moving at warp speed around the course. In parts, the organisers tell me, the course runs very narrow and through some awkward chicanes. They can't have someone running a wheelchair into the back of people's legs and blocking the runners' paths.

But Dick and Rick's example spurs me on and I explain that there are very few avenues that allow Thomas and me to participate in sport together – all other options are closed off.

Eventually they relent – they are parents too – and we are on.

The sportsfield of the Lord Williams's School in Thame is packed with runners when we arrive – some casual, sipping drinks in the shade and others more serious going through their running drills up and down the field. Georgie, Alice, my mum and dad have come with us, but as I unpack Thomas's wheelchair from the car and lift him out of his car seat into it, I suddenly feel very out of place.

This is a serious event, I think to myself. What the hell are you doing barging your way in here? You and Thomas don't belong here, you idiot.

We surreptitiously make our way to the cluster of runners forming near the start line. I pin my number to the front of my running shirt and do the same for Thomas: 704 and 705. I then attach the time-chip to his shoe and mine to my trainer.

There are one or two stares from the assembled runners – it's now patently obvious that the two of us intend to run with them and there are some old-fashioned looks shot in our direction. Again, I feel that we don't really belong here.

The pack of runners has now formed in anticipation of the starter's gun – the elite runners up front, fun runners in the middle and fatties and octogenarians at the back. We join the last of these groups. I have agreed with the organisers that I'll start at the back and only start to move through the field once the field stretches out. We're not here to win, we're simply here to participate.

The gun goes off and it's a few minutes before our group starts to move up. Eventually we start to plod gently forward up to and across the start line. Here goes!

The pace is steady at the back of the course. I'm happy to see I'm not the only one doing something out of the ordinary here – a group of firemen are jogging along in full regalia, including oxygen masks, helmets and tanks on their backs. It's going to get pretty sweaty in there in today's heat.

After a short while, we turn onto Thame High Street and there are crowds along the pavement, applauding the runners and urging them on. As we approach, I hear someone shout, 'Wow, amazing! C'mon the wheelchair!'

The hair stands up on the back of my neck. Yay, Thomas, we're doing this!

What an experience. And what amazing support as we run the course! Cheers much louder than anything I've ever experienced in any of my other sporting undertakings to date. Thomas is loving the attention.

Eventually the runners begin to thin out and Thomas and I

start to make our way forwards. After several miles, we leave the town and trot down a hill towards the village of Towersey. As we reach the bottom on the hill, a sudden bang.

I look down – the right front wheel of Thomas's chair has burst in the heat. We're less than halfway, but we're buggered if that's going to stop us. We start up again and the burst tyre rattles uncontrollably at the front of the chair. At least people will hear us coming, I tell myself.

We reach Towersey and it's up a short steep rise and on to the Phoenix Trail, a former railway track that runs between Thame and Princes Risborough. The course narrows here so we have to be a bit careful as we overtake.

'Give us a lift!' people call.

'Oh, no, overtaken by a wheelchair,' moans another.

On one occasion, Thomas's left arm spasms just as we are negotiating a narrow overtaking manoeuvre. His hands smacks loudly against the Lycra-clad right buttock of the woman we are overtaking. She turns in surprise and looks at me.

'Sorry!' I say as we pass and as I look at her face I realise with horror that she thinks it was me.

'Oh no,' I say, slowing down to her pace to explain. I point at Thomas. 'It was him.' And then I realise I'm putting the blame on my disabled son and that I now look even more of an idiot. We accelerate away. 'Thomas, behave yourself!' I shout to Tommy in front of me, who is grinning from ear to ear, seemingly enjoying his father's embarrassment.

After a while we return to the town and we wend our way through the streets and into the final mile.

As we turn the corner into the final straight back into the school playing fields, we see the finish line and a throng of supporters. 'And here comes James and his son Tom in the wheelchair'!' I hear them announcing over the tannoy. The crowd look and realise that something unusual is happening and a great cheer goes up.

I raise Thomas's arm as we cross the line and his face beams with delight.

I glimpse my family and see my dad, taller than the others, shouting and clapping, electrified with the emotion of the moment. I recognise the same delighted expression I had seen on his face in the photo of him when my nephew Oliver was born, the expression I had longed to see when my own kids came into this world. It's a look of unabated joy and pride and it brings home just how much this moment means for all of us, not just Thomas and me.

Oh shit, I suddenly think to myself, I'm actually crying. How did that happen? Why are you crying, you idiot?

For once, they're tears of unmitigated joy, but even so, I'm grateful for the sweat of exertion which is concealing the tears running down my face as our sporting dreams are finally fulfilled.

We find our way through the crowd to Georgie, Alice and my parents.

'He bloody beat me,' I joke. 'All my effort and he beat me across the line!'

Tommy is beaming, enjoying the attention and the experience of something new. He's six years old. Tell me what other six-year-olds have competed in a 10-kilometre with 1,000 other people. For the first time, Thomas has done something that his 'normal' peers have never done.

Afterwards I ponder how far we've come. It's not the way

TWO FOR JOY

I'd imagined it during those short months that I'd watched Georgie's belly expanding.

It is a different outcome to my dream.

But different is what it is.

Not worse.

Just different.

32. Extreme Sports

The success of the race has brought a new sense of impetus and we begin to realise that the only thing that's holding us back is our own imagination.

'Let's take them skiing!' I announce to Georgie one day.

She looks at me quizzically but knows better than to discount the idea out of hand.

'OK?' she answers. 'How's that going to work?'

'I've been doing some digging and I've come across an organisation called Disability Snowsport,' I reply. 'Look, here's their website. It says: "We work to make sure that anyone with a disability, may it be learning, sensory or physical, can ski or snowboard alongside other people." *Anyone*, it says.'

'They haven't met Thomas and Alice then, have they?!' says Georgie, only half-joking.

'There's a snow centre in Hemel Hempstead,' I continue. Hemel is only forty-five minutes from us. Now that the scales have fallen from my eyes in terms of what's possible for the twins, I have to admit I'm starting to feel that we have a lot of lost ground to make up. Abseiling, skiing, scuba-diving? Maybe not that last one . . .

'Fine, but how does it work?' Georgie says.

'I spoke to this really nice guy earlier,' I say.

'Oh, right,' she replies suspiciously.

'And he says that they have seats on skis which we strap the twins in to.'

'Yes, but we can't strap the twins into any old seats,' she says.

'I know,' I reply. 'I explained about the spasms. I just think we're going to have to try it and see how it goes.'

Georgie remains unconvinced.

I say, 'What's the worst that can happen?' which is a bit of a stupid question when you're about to undertake an extreme sport with a severely disabled child.

*

The Snow Centre at Hemel Hempstead looks like a huge aircraft hangar from the outside. Inside, they've done a fantastic job of bringing a slice of the Alps to this unglamorous corner of the Home Counties.

We meet our instructor, Nick, and he talks us through the apparatus and explains how it will work.

'Once the kids have their ski gear on, we'll put them into the sit-chairs, strap them in and then put the helmets on. All very straightforward,' he says. 'OK?'

I love the looks of blissful ignorance that the twins have on their faces at these moments. Too often recently, these faces have been in evidence just before an operation or some other hideous medical procedure. Then, those innocent smiles turn to panic as they realise what's about to happen, as the anaesthetist closes in with the mask or the nurse with the needle. Today, I hope, we'll see a different reaction.

'Our only worry is whether the seats will be comfortable enough,' Georgie says. 'The twins tend to have quite a lot of involuntary movement and so their wheelchairs are heavily padded.' She indicates the points of pressure around the twins in their chairs.

'Don't worry,' he says. 'We have these.' He brandishes a handful of large foam squares and rectangles.

OK, I think, a bit Heath Robinson, but let's do it.

We dress the twins quickly in their jackets, scarves and gloves and we're glad we have as we enter the arena itself and the temperature drops to -4°C.

Alice goes first and is loaded into the seat, strapped in and ready to go. The helmet covers her head and most of her eyes as well and she tilts her head back to look up at us from beneath the rim. She's smiling, playing the fool and enjoying the attention.

Alice's toboggan is attached to Nick, who is attached to the lift, and we're off up the slope. We gather at the top. Georgie, Nick and I on our skis, Alice wedged with pieces of yellow foam into her chariot. I ski down a few metres to watch her as she comes over the lip at the top of the hill.

Her face is a picture as she draws up to the ledge and looks down. She seems to be saying, 'Me? Down there? You have *got* to be kidding.'

Nick sets off with Alice in front of him and Georgie and I ski down in front, watching for the reaction on her face. Sheer terror to start with, but gradually a huge smile as the unfamiliar sensation becomes acceptable and she begins to realise that she is safe.

We reach the bottom and she's beaming now. Another couple of runs later and I can tell that she's addicted. We reach the bottom and she shouts 'Again!'

*

Buoyed by the success of the skiing trip, the irrepressible Kelly co-opts Laura, one of the twins' wonderful teachers from school, into taking the twins to a theme park during the summer holidays.

Kelly notices Alice eying up one particularly frightening-looking water ride. The screams as the kids come shooting down the water slide have attracted her to the possibility of another thrilling adventure.

'Do you want to go on that, Alice?' she asks.

Alice's face lights up and her body goes into excited spasm. Sometimes, these spasms are a good sign.

'All right then,' says Kelly and the four of them march up to the gate.

'Sorry, no wheelchairs,' says the guy operating the ride.

'Oh,' says Kelly. 'Why not?'

'If the boat gets stuck at the top of the chute, they have to be able to walk down on their own,' he explains.

'No problem,' says Kelly.

'Oh,' says the man, suddenly embarrassed that he seems to have underestimated these kids' abilities.

He eyes the kids suspiciously, presumably wondering exactly how these children are supposed to walk. He looks up at Kelly, whose face returns a 'what are you waiting for?' look.

'In which case that's fine,' he says, and on they go.

When they return home that evening, they are full of excitement about the day that they have had. Kelly shows us a photo of the twins' faces as they descend the water slide . . . a picture of rapturous joy.

33. Talk to Me

To see the twins enjoying life to the full is a vindication of the decisions the doctors made all those years ago – to give these children a chance at life and to allow them to experience all of its glories and shortcomings.

Even so, for all that these achievements represent wonderful breakthroughs; they have all been activities in which the twins have been passive participants. Yes, they have loved every second of the thrill of the running, the skiing or the theme park, but they have been inactively involved rather than doing it themselves.

At the same time, I'd always imagined that life would get progressively harder for us as a family as the twins got bigger. Already, at six, they are starting to get heavy. But the truth is, life is getting so much better now: their personalities are starting to shine.

Over time, I begin to realise that I like the twins enormously as people. Of course, I've always loved them – sometimes with an intensity that would bring the sky down – but as their characters reveal themselves, so I become proud not just of their bravery and ability to survive everything that's thrown at them, but also proud of the individuals they are becoming.

Communication is becoming easier for them and as it does, we get to know our children better and their qualities become more evident. Suddenly the time we spent searching for the right school and the hours spent agonising over whether or not to go ahead with surgery look like they are paying dividends.

For Thomas, communication is harder than for his sister, owing to his deafness and general preference for arsing about, like any young boy. He is the class clown. Anyone who knows him and who knows his history can't help but have their hearts melt when he beams at them. He's not sparing with his smiles, he applies them liberally, whenever the opportunity presents itself, which, when you think about it, is pretty much all the time.

Except funerals perhaps, but generally, he's got the right idea.

I think back to the little boy we seemed to be losing just a few years ago – sliding into his own shell because he couldn't hear anything and because he found it so hard to connect with the world around him. He's come such a long way.

The irony is that his mouth control is much better than his sister's. If it wasn't for his hearing impairment, we have no doubt that his speech would be better than it is. As it is, he has very little in the way of words, but he is starting to indicate choice through throwing his voice when asked a question, to indicate yes.

I'm at work one morning when Georgie forwards me a video

of Thomas that Dr Lin has recorded on his phone during an assessment. The scene depicts Georgie sitting face to face with Thomas in his wheelchair.

'One,' she begins patiently, holding up her index finger to indicate the British Sign Language sign for 'one'.

'Wuh,' Tommy repeats slowly and in his lap I see his left hand mimic the sign – his index finger leaving the rest of his fisted fingers to point, independently, to the floor.

'Two,' Georgie says slowly, making the V-sign for 'two'. (Careful where you use that sign in public.)

'Ooh,' he replies and his middle fingers curls out slowly to join the index finger.

'Good boy, three,' she says now, the ring finger now joining the other two.

'Hee,' replies Thomas and again his hand moves to mimic his mother's.

'Great, Thomas,' I hear Dr Lin's voice behind the camera.

I'm sitting at my desk, quietly willing him to complete the task, to make it to ten. I realise that I'm chewing my nails in a rather un-office like manner. I sit on my hands now. My heart is thumping.

'Four,' continues Georgie.

Same response. And for five, six, seven, eight, nine.

'Ten,' Georgie says finally, shaking her open hand in front of her face to signal the number.

'Eh,' Thomas replies triumphantly and holds his hand open in his lap. He grins from ear to ear.

'Yes!' I shout at the screen. He did it!

Quizzical heads pop up around the office, like meerkats from their burrows.

'Sorry,' I apologise to their quizzical faces. Admittedly, the act of counting to ten is not going to win Thomas any *Guinness Book of Records* awards, but for him this was his marathon, his Iron Man, his Nobel Prize-winning effort. It makes me so happy to think that he is finally on the right track. This is just the beginning, think what he might accomplish with his hands and with his voice if this sort of progress is maintained.

*

At school they have developed communication books for the twins. These are large, bound A4 books with acetate pages depicting symbols. The twins use their eyes to select particular symbols on the page and to navigate around the book from page to page. Alice has become particularly adept with hers. While most other movements in her body are virtually impossible to control effectively, she has a good level of control over her eyes.

Perhaps Hortensia was right – great things are becoming possible.

Alice's eye-pointing skills have led the school to successfully apply to the Local Authority to provide her with an eye gaze computer. This is a screen that stands on a mount on the table. At the bottom of the screen there is a camera which detects where on the page Alice's eyes are looking. She might be looking at a picture of a yoghurt on one side of the screen and cereal on the other. The camera will detect what she is looking at, and in doing so, she can choose which she would prefer to eat for her breakfast.

I had no idea how much progress she had been making with this device until she and Georgie come to visit Thomas and me in hospital on one of his long-term admissions.

'Alice has a surprise for you, Tommy,' Georgie says, reaching into the bag behind Alice's chair. Alice suddenly brightens. 'She's written you a letter. Shall I read it to you?'

Georgie begins to read,

> Dear Tinker,
> You are my brother, I miss you. I would like you to come home. Are you lying down? It has been snowing. Christmas is soon. Father Christmas is coming. I would like to visit you. I am excited. I want to play outside and go swimming with you.
>
> I love you,
> Alice xxx

'Wow! She wrote that?' I say.

'On her eye gaze computer,' Georgie replies. 'With Laura at school.'

I'm utterly gobsmacked. I had no idea that Alice had developed this skill to such an extent.

Her speech is coming through now as well, thanks to the painstaking efforts of the Speech and Language therapists, teachers and conductors in her class at PACE, led by the indomitable Josie. She can't be easily understood by people who do not know her, but by those who do, phrases like 'chocolate cake', 'Strictly Come Dancing' and 'X Factor' are all part of her daily vocabulary. I hope to myself that her vocabulary might extend one day to more cerebral matters, but for now, just those words are music to my ears.

One night I am once again going through the normal ritual of putting her to bed. After I brush her teeth, brush her hair, give her her overnight medicines (just five syringes – nothing like her brother's intake) and read her a story, I tuck her up into bed. I lean in to kiss her and, as usual, I tell her I love her.

As always, she looks up to me silently, telling me with her eyes that the love is reciprocated. And then, with huge force of effort, she lifts her head from the pillow and tries to speak. There's a look of determination on her face as she struggles with the effort of shaping her mouth to form the right words, of coordinating her breathing to provide a column of air upwards and outwards to carry her words. These tiny things – second nature to all of us – require so much intense focus for her. She battles to overcome the conflicting messages being sent by her brain and then, finally, she whispers in faltering, stuttering breaths:

'I. Love. You. Daddy.'

She giggles as she sees tears start to form in my eyes, delighted with herself that she has been able to convey this sentiment and to trigger this reaction from her ridiculous, soppy father.

34. Boy Racer

Seeing the twins progress to such a positive extent makes us begin to wonder what else might be achievable for them. Doors which were previously closed to them now swing open. The hand control that they have learned at school opens up the possibilities in a new world: independent mobility.

It is becoming increasingly clear that the lack of independence is frustrating for the twins. Too often we've dismissed this desire for independence with the platitude, 'Yes, but they've never known any different,' but we also recognise that for children as intelligent as them, it must be frustrating seeing the rest of the world operating in such a different manner to them. Even though they are beginning to express choice they have no real say in *where* they go.

They go everywhere in their buggies. They are strapped into them when they wake up in the morning, they are fed their breakfast in them, they are taken to school in them and they go shopping in them. Everywhere they go, they are pushed by someone else, someone who dictates where they go in the world and what they see.

There are times when the four of us might be on a walk and Georgie and I might stop to admire the view behind us. We have to remind ourselves that the twins hear our conversation, but can't turn to view the scene themselves. We have to remember to turn the buggies around as well in order for them to be able to see what we are talking about. It's these simple things that the twins are so reliant on others for.

An important element of their future independence will depend on their ability to get from A to B under their own steam, and gaining some level of hand control opens up this opportunity.

We hear about a wonderful charity called Whizz-Kidz, which provides powered wheelchairs to families like ours. If we can find a way to enable the twins to control these chairs, then independent movement could become a reality. But we enter into the discussion cautiously, as it's hard to see how the twins will be able to control a wheelchair, with such limited physical control. The twins have an assessment to determine what types of chairs and controls will suit them best.

The main question is: how are we going to get the twins to make the devices move in the intended direction? Thomas's hand control is improving, so the team from Whizz-Kidz agree that we should try him with a joystick. Alice finds hand control harder, so they recommend that we use a single switch which she will be able to use to move the chair forwards and backwards.

After several months, the chairs arrive at our house. They

don't look much – lumpy black boxes on grey wheels. They are wheeled from the back of the delivery van onto our drive and then we attach the twins' indoor seating systems on to the top of these bases. We carry the twins across and load them into their seats.

Once the settings are established to everyone's satisfaction, they're off.

Alice is steady Eddie. She requires some help in reaching for the switch, but when she does find it, she's enjoying the sensation of controlling the device and the new feeling of her chair bumping along across the driveway and lawn.

Thomas takes a while to grasp the concept but eventually he understands and his face is one of grim determination as he wrestles to grasp the joystick to propel the machine in the right direction. With huge effort, he grabs at it and the machine jerks forward. His face lights up with the sensation of self-propulsion and as he loses concentration for a second, his grip slips from the control. He looks down again and brings his arm around in a large arc until it hits the controls again. He's off.

Here he is, through sheer force of will, applying every functioning neural synapse in his largely function-free brain, to the simple, tiny task of controlling the joystick. Each time his hand slips from the control it seems to take Herculean effort to put it back there – I can see his forehead is glistening with sweat now – but the incentive of free will is proving too strong.

It's as if his entire life has been building up to this moment – every needle, every scar, every second of endless, mind-numbing therapy – it's all been for this moment. Everything he has learnt, all of the strategies he has taught himself for dealing with his disadvantage, now come together in a laser-like focus to enable him to undertake this simple task. The spasms of his dystonia scream at him to fail, to flail his arms about uselessly, but his focus will not be bent. It's like a shard of bright light bursting from the darkness that has shadowed so much of his life to date.

He careers off into the flower bed!

I walk over to him and bring him back to the safety of the driveway. No sooner have I done that than he is off again, crashing back towards the borders. The wheelchair lurches like a First World War tank as it crosses from the edge of the lawn into the flower bed.

'Thomas, no!' I shout too late as a large pink geranium bush disappears beneath his front wheels.

Thomas is in fits of giggles.

I'm laughing too. Every time I tell him what to do, pointing where I want him to go, he shoots off in the opposite direction. I realise, with pride, that this is the first time in his life that he's been able to so openly disobey me. Disobedience – the stock in trade of every seven-year-old boy – has been buried by circumstance all these years. Now Thomas finally has the opportunity to express it, to express his desire to do precisely what he wants, rather than what we want.

The game continues for an hour and a half, until it's time to go inside for tea. I switch off the main control at the back of the chair and flick the brake on. Thomas continues to urgently try to manoeuvre the joystick, while I start to unbuckle him from the chair. He looks up at me in desperation as he realises that the game is over. He bursts into tears.

'Wow!' I laugh at Thomas, 'You really love your new wheelchair, don't you?'

35. The Court of Public Opinion

We have agreed to take part in an interview with the *Mail on Sunday*.

The subject matter is premature babies and whether or not it is right to keep extremely premature babies alive when there is a chance that they end up being disabled.

To me it seems very simple as I look at my children and feel the love they are capable of giving and smiles and laughter they are capable of sharing. But this life is not without its challenges and I'm interested to see the conclusions that the article draws. What I'm certain of though, is that everyone will understand our point of view and empathise with the difficulty of our position.

How wrong can you be? How stupid of me to think that.

Just last week Georgie was out walking with the twins and bumped into a lady in the village. She said, 'Wow! Aren't the twins looking terrific?'

Georgie beamed.

'Amazing to think that they were only little blobs when you first arrived here!' she said.

Blobs? Thanks.

The day of the interview arrives and I speak to the journalist. She asks about the early days and I open up with the whole story – the full nine yards – including the difficult decision we made not to have Thomas resuscitated if he dipped again. And then she says, 'There are those who feel that children like yours ought not to be kept alive, because the cost to the state and to families like yours – financially and emotionally – is such a huge burden.'

It's the first time anyone has openly challenged our twins' right to life and I feel a growing sense of panic that this article might take a turn for the worse. More importantly, I feel a sudden uncertainty about whether we have done the wrong thing in fighting so hard for their survival.

'What do you say to those people?' she asks.

My stomach turns. 'I understand that this is a difficult debate, and I can see both sides,' I reply, buying time with platitudes. Then, I say, 'But I object to the argument that these babies are second-class citizens, less deserving of NHS resources and a chance to live than, say, a young mother with cancer or someone who has been paralysed in a car accident. Don't say that our children are less worthy.'

'OK,' she replies. 'But what about the quality of the life that they lead?'

I say, 'Over the long term our experience has been very positive. We love them being alive. And, more importantly, they themselves love being alive.'

But suddenly I'm not so sure any more. They absolutely spend more of their lives being happy than going through suffering. Don't they?

Sunday comes around and I look up the piece online. There in the centre of the paper is the article:

'Two pieces of research raise a profoundly troubling question . . . Is it sometimes wrong to keep premature babies alive?'

The article raises all of the questions one would expect about the whys and wherefores of keeping such fragile babies alive and she has done a nice job with our story, telling it accurately and fairly and putting across my point of view. No, the article is fine.

I start scrolling through the comments from readers at the bottom. There are eighty-four comments! Some lovely messages of support from people who admire the way our family has contended with the dramas we have faced. And then it all starts to go a bit wrong . . .

> Jackie, Scotland
> Last week I watched adults with dreadful physical and mental difficulties in a cafe. Carers had to feed them and clean up their dribble. I'm sorry if that description offends anyone but tell me what kind of life is that for a human being? Sometimes nature should not be tampered with – just because medical science makes something possible doesn't always make it right.

> JD, St Albans UK
> They are alive because of medical advances, or as

I would put it doctors playing god, the world is overpopulated now, and most of the worlds children are starving, it's obscene!

Christine, London, England
Sometimes a baby is not supposed to be born. Nature makes a mistake. Just because we have the technology does not mean we should use it every single time. To have a child knowing it will be severely disabled is selfish. Quality of life is vital. I know many may disagree with me. But this is what I believe.

Katie, Peterborough
Why would anyone deliberatly bring a disabled Child into the world? What life will they have? If you can't concieve or go full term, just accept your body is telling you that you can;t have children

I feel my temperature rising. Who are these small-minded idiots with their splenetic, misguided opinions?

Some of them can't even spell! The grammar is awful!

What have we done with the Internet, allowing these ignorant dickheads the right to stand in judgement when they can't even fucking spell or construct a sensible or grammatically correct sentence?

What have we done!?

I start typing my response.

Then I delete it all.

Then I type it again.

Again and again, to tell them they're wrong, that they have no idea what the fuck they're talking about.

Then I slap the laptop closed and storm out of the room.

'Going for a walk!' I shout to Georgie as I slam the front door behind me.

*

Several days later, I'm playing football for Fenway Park. This is one of those occasions when everything is going our way as a team – we gallop into an early 2–0 lead and the striker I am marking is struggling to make an impact, chiefly because the ball seems to be spending a lot of time in his own half. He is a tough looking diminutive Scot.

As is the way with strikers, nothing is his fault, it is the fault of the service being supplied by midfield and, in his eyes, the calamitous defending which means that they are down by two goals.

'You fucking useless spastic!' he shouts at his central defender as the third goal goes in.

Now, as you might imagine, I'm not a massive fan of this particular word. And I'm still reeling from some of the ignorant comments about the *Mail* article.

'Oi!' I shout. 'Come here.'

I beckon him over, pointing to the ground in front of me as if summoning a dog.

'Wha'?' he says, eyes bulging.

'Er, look,' I say, suddenly unsure of myself. 'Listen, we don't use that sort of language nowadays.'

'Oh. Don't we?' He replies nastily. His face is stretched with the effort of trying not to hit me. 'What's it to you, you ponce?'

This is going well . . .

'My two disabled children is what it's got to do with me,' I reply. 'They are what you might call "spastics".'

The fury disappears from his face. Everyone within earshot looks embarrassed by the awkwardness of the situation,

He shrugs his shoulders, mutters under his breath – was that an apology? – and turns to the centre circle to kick off again.

The ball moves slowly back towards their defence as our strikers and midfield press forward. Our tails are up and we're eager for more goals. The ball is eventually ferried towards the very same 'spastic' centre half, who rather unglamorously stands on the ball and falls over. Our striker sniffs the opportunity, steals the ball and thumps it past the helpless keeper.

To my right, I'm aware of my Scottish friend bristling. He throws up his arms in desperation.

'You fucking, useless . . .' he pauses, 'CUNT!'

He looks to me, smiling.

'Much better,' I say. 'Thank you.'

*

Our tenth wedding anniversary is approaching and my saintly parents bravely agree to take the twins on for a week, while we escape to Morocco for a much-needed rest.

'It's time for you to celebrate as a couple,' Mum says. 'After all you've been through, take some time, rest up and just be a couple. Enjoy the fact that everyone is well and make the most of it.'

After two days amid the hubbub, colours and smells of Marrakech, we escape to a hilly retreat in the Atlas Mountains. Given the rarity of these escapes, no expense has been spared and we arrive at the hotel and are ushered to our private Moroccan tent, complete with four-poster bed, roll-topped bath and, best of all, its own veranda and mini pool. The view from our veranda looks across to the hills along the other side of the valley.

We spend an idle four days here in this sanctuary, just reading by the pool, eating indecent amounts of food and occasionally belly-flopping into the pool when the heat gets too much.

On the night of the date of our anniversary itself, I have arranged a private dinner on a balcony overlooking the rest of the resort. We have already had a bottle of champagne in our room and now more champagne is brought us, compliments of the hotel.

'Oh well, rude not to,' says Georgie.

There is no menu for us. Instead, the head chef visits our table and says we can have whatever we want. The food arrives a little later, with yet more wine, and is spectacular. We clink our glasses and I raise a toast to our ten years, drinking in Georgie's beauty after all these years and tribulations.

Eventually, inevitably, the talk turns to the twins. I'm still agitated about the comments which followed the *Mail* article.

'I just . . .' I'm afraid to admit it to Georgie.

'What?' she says.

'I just. I dunno. I just struggle with the notion that people think they ought not to have been kept alive,' I say.

'I know,' she replies.

'But at the end of the day, is it all worth it, for the suffering, the pain and the frustrations of their disability?' I say. 'Is it worth it for everything they have to go through?'

And then Georgie says something really quite fantastic.

'I'm pretty sure being happy is more important than being able-bodied.'

She pauses.

'Think about it, J. The alternative was nothing – an endless black hole. I think you'll find they're pretty bloody happy about being given the opportunity to experience life.'

Of course she's right. This amazing, strong woman, who hasn't just carried the twins to the pinnacle of their achievements, she's carried me as well.

After dinner, we return to our tent and undress. We giggle like school kids as we run, naked, through the darkness, across the veranda and jump into our swimming pool. We lie side by side in the water, staring up at the stars, and I wonder drunkenly how life could possibly get any better.

36. A Life Magnified

Dad and I have agreed to meet for dinner after work.

He asks after the family and, after the usual updates, he opens up a more intricate subject matter.

'I remember you once saying that being a dad to disabled kids isn't necessarily worse than my experience of being a dad, just that it's different,' he says. 'Do you still think that's true?'

'Yes, absolutely,' I reply almost automatically.

'It's just that your experience has looked a whole lot worse than mine in recent years,' he says.

I laugh. 'Yes, fair dos, although your children are pretty exceptional.'

He groans.

I think for a minute, then say, 'The truth is this crazy situation isn't easy to define. There's no point trying to pigeonhole it as wonderful or dreadful because it's neither . . . and both.'

'Are you both happy?' he asks.

'Yes, we are. That's what people struggle to see. I can tell people don't believe me and that's fine. I read somewhere that one in ten people don't believe it. They imagine that it's impossible for parents of disabled kids to be happy. You think I'm being brave, but I'm not, we really are happy. What looks so awful to you is ordinary to us.

'I mean sometimes it just seems too odd for words. The little things, like the fact that Georgie has to carry screwdrivers and spanners in amongst the Estée Lauder make-up in her handbag in case she needs to do running repairs on one of the twins' wheelchairs. Like the fact that we have syringes lying about the house or the fact that we can never go for long coastal walks, because we can't lift the wheelchairs over stiles or gates.

'Hands up – I didn't know whether I could cope at the start. I hated it, I'll be honest, I really struggled with my anger. When we got the diagnosis I was blinded by grief, I could only concentrate on what they wouldn't be able to do. But as the years have passed, I've started to realise that we have to focus on what they *can* achieve and how to make the most of that.

'From the chaos came order: a different kind of order and one which probably looks totally ludicrous to anyone looking in, but an order that keeps the system chugging along.'

He looks thoughtful. 'I read the *Mail* piece,' he says eventually.

'Oh right,' I say defensively. I'm still stinging a bit from that.

'What did you make of the comments, especially the ones saying that it would have been better if Thomas and Alice hadn't been resuscitated?' he asks. 'All that stuff about the cost to society and families – emotionally and financially . . .' he trails off hesitantly, clearly aware that this is something of a sore point.

'Bullshit,' I reply crossly. 'And not just because they are my children and I love them as passionately as any parent. It's because I believe that they have the potential to make a bigger contribution to society than anyone else I know. I realise that sounds peculiar when the cost of keeping them alive is so massive, but they tell us all such an important story every single day that they keep battling and smiling. They teach all of us perspective – something we seem to have lost sight of. If they're happy, why the hell aren't the rest of us? We're so lucky to have had this experience and to have these lessons brought to us every day.'

'So, you wouldn't change it if you had the chance?' he asks.

'I honestly don't think I would,' I say, holding my hands out. 'It's a life magnified: the lows are much lower than you could probably imagine and they are long and sustained. But the highs, wow, the highs, they make it all worthwhile.'

'I can kind of understand that,' he says.

I'm not sure he does, so continue, 'Look – so, I'll never teach Thomas how to bowl a cricket ball properly. But I hold him in my arms and we hold the bat together as Uncle Rupert bowls him dolly drops on Frinton beach. And OK, Alice and I will never glide around the dance floor together on her twenty-first birthday, but I hold her tight as we dance around the kitchen to Bruno Mars and she giggles like an idiot.

'We can still do whatever we want, but it just takes a lot more effort and determination to do the simple things.'

'Well, I don't know how you do it,' he says, 'and always with a smile on your faces.'

'We have to keep smiling, Dad. Because they do. Their lives are a lot tougher than ours. These kids of ours are so charming, so caring, so delightful – their megawatt smiles are like lighthouses in the dark on bad days. When we wheel them through the shopping centre and people stare, I feel nothing but huge pride because I know what they've overcome to be here. And I see the way my twins trust and love and laugh and I know that they are better human beings than I can ever hope to be. They show us the way. They show us how to keep going.'

He smiles as I burble on.

'We've been faced with some pretty harsh situations, some awful decisions, but that puts hairs on your chest. It focuses the mind. We're forced to focus on what really matters, on what is most important to us. Everything else seems just a bit uneventful. This situation gives us a purpose in our lives that reaches far beyond anything we've had to deal with before. It's all about love: a love that drives you onwards, whatever the odds, to win for your child.'

I stop. Aware that I'm blustering now.

'Sorry,' I say. 'I'm ranting.' I pause. 'I just wish people were more accepting of disability and less frightened of it. I wish people would see the person rather than the wheelchair, see the ability rather than the disability. I think our story is important because it shows how far the twins have come and what they're capable of.'

'Maybe you should write a book about it,' he jokes.

'Haha . . . maybe I should!' I reply.

PART 4

THREE FOR
A GIRL

37. An Indian Summer

It's springtime.

Georgie calls me from the kitchen with a wobble in her voice, 'J, can you come here, please?'

Sounds ominous, I think to myself. 'Coming!' I call.

I enter the kitchen. Georgie is shaking.

'What's the matter?' I ask, worried.

'I think I'm pregnant,' she says and bursts into tears.

I cross the room and wrap my arms around her. Impossible, I tell myself. We had been told that we would never conceive naturally, that we were incompatible as partners. And yet, miracles do happen. We know that now, better than most.

My heart is beating so hard with excitement at the news. Georgie's head rests against my chest and I'm pretty sure its hammering has given the game away long before I open my mouth.

I start with a question as we break the embrace and stand looking into one another's eyes: 'Are you OK?'

'Yes, yes, I'm fine,' she replies.

'What do you think?' I ask.

'I don't know, J.' She starts to sob again.

After what happened with the first pregnancy and Georgie's concern, however misguided, that she was somehow at fault, the need for her to go into the unknown again weighs understandably heavily on her.

The memories of those awful days, seven years ago, when her pregnancy had gone so spectacularly wrong, have never gone, but they have been somewhat buried by the day-to-day exertions of having to care for the twins.

But now those memories come bubbling back to the surface, prompting unanswerable questions like What if it happens again? Will the pregnancy go to full term? Is it safe?

*

After several weeks of deliberation, we come to the same conclusion: this is a blessing, a sibling for our twins. Never mind us, they deserve this.

And so the die is cast. We decide to press on.

Given our history, we are referred to a service at the John Radcliffe hospital in Oxford, which ensures that we will be closely monitored through the pregnancy. The lead consultant is a man called Lawrence Impey. His clipped tone camouflages a strong sense of compassion.

On one of our early appointments with him we find ourselves without care support so we take the twins along with us.

Alice giggles as her mother gets undressed and we see the

same look on Mr Impey's face that we have seen on so many others who come into contact with the twins. It's a look of delight as he realises that despite the outer frame of disability, a normal cheeky girl lies inside.

After the meeting, as we are leaving, he says, 'Don't worry, I will do everything I can to make sure everything is all right for you,' and it's clear that the twins have made their mark.

We wait until we are four months into the pregnancy before we tell anyone. When we tell my mum, she looks shocked but delighted.

Later, when Georgie is out of earshot, she says, 'I'm just amazed that you both had the energy for . . . you know . . . that!'

And we laugh conspiratorially at the seeming impossibility of it.

*

Several months later I catch the train up to Oxford. It's our twenty-week scan at the John Radcliffe and after the 'excitements' and general lack of preparedness around the twins' birth, this time we're leaving nothing to chance and we are going to find out the sex. In this way, we won't be caught out on the name, since we'll have plenty of time to choose. It also makes sense to be able to tell the twins whether they should expect a brother or a sister.

Georgie's expanding midriff speaks daily of the miracle that has been bestowed on us and amidst all the trepidation as we approach the twenty-four-week mark, we thank our lucky stars for this news.

The scanning room at the hospital is a carbon copy of the room where we first heard that Georgie was pregnant with twins, now seven years ago. Once again, I perch alongside the bed and grasp Georgie's hand as the lights are dimmed and we peer at the screen.

The scan shows a beautiful baby girl growing exactly as she should be inside Georgie – the right size, the right shape, all the legs and arms and no signs of anything wrong at this stage. A girl! My heart swells with pride. My mind is already racing ahead to the possibilities of what she will be like.

'You do realise this means we're going to have to stop swearing in front of the kids,' I say. One of the secret delights of having children with limited speech is that you can swear as much as you like in front of them without fear of those words being repeated in socially awkward situations.

'You swear too much anyway.' Georgie smiles. 'It'll be good for you.'

She raises her eyebrows at the nurse, who smiles and says, 'All in order. Can you wait outside, they'll call you for the cervical scan in a minute.'

The scan of the cervix is a simple formality for people with a history like ours. We are pleased that they are taking extra steps to ensure that everything is OK. The added reassurance of having regular checks provides us with the confidence to try to enjoy the pregnancy more than would otherwise be the case.

We enter another scanning room. A new nurse introduces herself, asks Georgie to undress and within a minute is inserting a probe. Not for the first time I think how bizarre it must be to be a woman: 'Good morning, I'm Janice, just going to pop this in' – all within a minute of meeting.

'Is that door locked?' Georgie asks the nurse. The bottom of the bed points directly at the door.

'Er,' replies the nurse in place of 'no', which is what she actually means.

I jump up and turn the lock and we all laugh.

The nurse's smiles turn to a frown as she considers the information presented to her on the screen. Is something wrong? I smile uneasily and squeeze Georgie's hand. The look on her face is more meaningful than the unintelligible patterns on the screen.

'Just going to get a doctor,' she says, unlocking and then bolting out of the door.

I stand, reach for a towel and drape it across Georgie's naked hips.

'Oh God,' says Georgie. 'What's going on?

I shrug, stumped, and the door opens as a new doctor enters the room and briefly introduces herself before reinserting the probe.

'Hmm,' she says.

Hmm, I think. Care to elaborate?

She points to the screen and says, 'This is your cervix, the structure which holds the baby in place during pregnancy until the time is right.' She indicates a thin, grey shape on the screen.

'At your last check, you had about six centimetres of cervix holding the baby in. This has reduced to about nine millimetres now; as you can see, it's very thin. In other words, your cervix is about to begin dilating.'

'What does that mean?' Georgie asks.

She replies, with a grave expression, 'I'd say there is now a seventy-five per cent chance that your baby will deliver in the next four weeks.'

The tingle of heightened anxiety once again spreads through

my body. This familiar feeling of fight or flight returns and the adrenalin surges through my veins. It's an experience I wish we didn't have to go through, but now I think about it I don't think I ever feel more alert or more alive than at these times of confrontation.

'We have twins,' I explain. 'They were born at twenty-four weeks and they are both severely disabled. What can we do to prevent that from happening again?'

This doesn't look like the sort of question she is 100 per cent comfortable with – understandably – we're not your average family. I can see her brain whirring as she considers the implications. Eventually she says, 'I'll get Lawrence to talk to you.'

We are shepherded to an office, where we stare at one another. There is nothing to say. No reassurances that will have any effect. Georgie's heard them too many times and so often they've been a triumph of hope over the crushing reality of the situation.

*

Lawrence Impey arrives. I present the issues to him as we see them – I want him to understand what he already knows, that this isn't an ordinary situation and that we shouldn't be categorised and treated in the same way as a normal family.

'Given all of that, is there any reasonable alternative to termination?' I say. 'The risks of continuing seem so high. I'm proud of the life that we have made for the twins, but I don't think that another disabled sibling is in the best interests of anyone, least of all the twins. I don't think our family can cope with the possibility of another disability.'

He pauses, pensive, waiting to ensure that I have finished. When he's certain I've said my piece, he raises his eyebrows as if seeking permission to speak.

I nod and he begins, 'Georgie, you have an incompetent cervix.'

Once again, I can't help wondering at the bizarre language that medics use.

'So this is what we are going to do,' he continues. 'We are going to put stitches into the cervix, which will have the effect of closing it up and keeping the baby on board. Normally, I would only put one stitch in, but I think in this case we will leave nothing to chance, so I'm going to put three in. This will significantly improve the chances of your baby staying put for a longer period. Hopefully through to term.'

'Hopefully?' Georgie repeats.

'There is an outside chance that it could bring on premature labour, but we are looking at extreme prematurity even if we do nothing. It makes sense to do this, even if it does cause the labour to start, because if it goes wrong, the end result is the same anyway.'

'What are the chances of it going wrong?' I ask.

'Our research shows that when the stitch does trigger premature labour, it does so before twenty-four weeks. There is less than a five per cent chance of anything going wrong in the critical period between twenty-four and twenty-eight weeks. If it comes sooner, the outcome is a foregone conclusion. Any later and we have a fighting chance of things being fine for the baby.'

He pauses.

'I know this is a hard situation for you and you must think very carefully about your decision.'

*

The next day, we are back at the John Radcliffe for the stitches. Do we really have any choice? Not for the first time, I feel like a small sailing boat far out at sea, buffeted by the waves of circumstance, its fate entirely in the hands of whatever weather God has decreed.

At least we now know why the twins came so early. Back at the start, no one had been able to put their finger on why Georgie's contractions had started so early, but now we know. Imagine if we hadn't been having regular checks with this pregnancy? We were, almost certainly, heading in exactly the same direction. I suddenly feel very grateful for Mr Impey's intervention.

Georgie undresses and wraps the surgical gown around her small, domed midriff. We are ushered into the theatre and I have a horrible sense of flashback as the epidural is administered to Georgie's spine to anaesthetise the lower half of her body. She leans back on the bed and within a short time the anaesthetic is kicking in.

She gasps in shock as her legs are lifted upwards towards her head.

'What?' She exclaims. 'Whose legs are those?'

The nurse is laughing. 'They're yours!' she says. 'The wonder of anaesthetics.'

Within minutes the procedure has been completed and Georgie has three staples stitched into her cervix.

Now all we need her to do is sit still for the next four months . . . no small challenge for the world's busiest woman.

38. Same, Same ...

Keeping Georgie still for four months always seemed as though it would be asking too much and so it proves.

Several weeks after the stitches the phone on my desk rings. It's Georgie, speaking through faltering breaths.

'Can you come, J?' she says.

'Are you OK?' I ask.

'I just fell over around the back of the house. I banged my head on the concrete.'

'God, are you OK?'

'J, I've got labour pains,' she says. 'Mr Impey told me to come in as quickly as possible so they can observe me.'

'Oh no,' I say.

'Can you meet me at the hospital?' she says.

My mind goes back to the fateful day seven years ago, when Georgie rang me to ask exactly the same thing. I can't believe this is happening all over again.

SAME, SAME . . .

*

Midnight two days later.

I sit by the bed clutching Georgie's hand. Once again she has been given drugs to open our baby's lungs to prepare for her early arrival.

The labour pains are coming in consistent waves now and the arrival of our little girl seems imminent.

As before, the drugs are causing Georgie drowsiness and sickness and she seems to fade in and out as I sit with her. My eyes sting. How can we be here again?

A knock at the door and in bustles a doctor from the neonatal intensive care unit. The midwife has asked him to come and visit us to explain what happens next.

His eyes tell the story of a busy night and possibly a busy day before that. He begins, 'I'm sorry to hear that things have taken a turn for the worse.'

'Thank you,' we say.

'I'm afraid it's very difficult to judge with any kind of certainty what direction things will go in for your baby once it arrives.'

'She,' Georgie interjects.

'Sorry,' he says, 'once she arrives. What is almost certain is that she will need to spend some time here in the hospital at the NICU. That stands for neonatal intensive care unit and it's the place where we look after the smallest and sickest newborn children.'

Georgie and I glance at one another. Has no one told him?

He continues, too tired to pick up the obvious signals from our quizzical looks. 'The likelihood is that the baby will require a significant amount of intervention on arrival – she will be placed into an incubator and will need medication and breathing apparatus in the early weeks.'

'Sorry,' I interject eventually. 'Hasn't anyone told you?'

'Told me what?' he replies.

'We've done this before,' I explain. 'We have twins who were born seven years ago at twenty-four weeks. They spent nine months in NICU.'

'Oh, right,' he says. 'I'm sorry, I had no idea.'

'No problem,' I continue. 'But the twins are severely disabled. Given that, do you think it's a sensible idea for us to be resuscitating this child at all?'

'What stage are you at?' he asks.

'Twenty-five weeks and three days,' replies Georgie.

'Well in that case, I'm afraid we have to resuscitate,' he says.

'What do you mean "have to"?' I ask aggressively. I'm tired too.

'The rules of this hospital dictate that every effort must be made to save any child born here past twenty-five weeks.' He explains.

'Is that sensible?' I ask again. 'Do you think that's the right choice for our family? We are struggling to deal with the heavy burden we already have on our plate. I'm not sure another disabled child is something we'd be able to deal with . . .'

'I see your point,' he says eventually. 'Look, this isn't a decision I'm permitted to make on my own. I'm afraid this is something which will have to be considered by the Ethics Committee of our hospital.'

He pauses, then says, 'Is that what you're asking me to do?'

I look at Georgie then back at the doctor.

'Yes,' I reply eventually. 'I think the conversation needs to be had.'

*

SAME, SAME . . .

For two more days, Georgie struggles with the labour pains. I'm trying to remain realistic about the outcome here. The memories of seven years ago are suddenly ever present in my thoughts, the deep dread that we are about to go through the same sorry episode all over again. Will we be strong enough? Will I be able to catch Georgie again this time? Will the grief overwhelm us if the unthinkable happens?

Two days and still no word back from the Ethics Committee. Evidently they need time to consider the unusual situation.

We sit and wait for the white smoke from their chimney, increasingly conscious that someone is going to have to make a decision any time now anyway.

*

Time ticks slowly past, every additional hour is a victory now. Georgie lies still in her hospital bed, her face etched with the agony of the pains and the misery of the thought of not completing the task of taking this pregnancy to term.

I spend the hours in the cubicle on the ward sitting with her, discussing our predicament, still focusing on our dreams for our daughter, should she make it.

I'm just a bystander, Georgie's assistant at best. I bring her food from the cafeteria downstairs – an endless stream of sandwiches, crisps and Cokes. Sometimes she feels strong enough to eat, but mostly she remains focused on the task at hand. She has gone into lockdown again, no emotion, just a single-minded focus on getting the job done. I feel I'm as much use as an ashtray on a motorbike, but I want to be here, supporting Georgie however I can.

*

Over the next two days, the contractions begin to reduce and Georgie's strength starts to return. After a week in hospital, she is released home.

She is under strict instruction to remain in bed for as much time as possible and following this recent scare we are following doctor's orders to a T.

39. . . . But Different

The thirtieth of November.

The day has finally come, the day neither of us ever thought we'd ever see. The due date has arrived, a full thirty-eight weeks after our little girl was conceived. Thirty-eight weeks! It felt like such a distant and unachievable target during those dark days and nights just a few months ago now.

The snow has been falling for the past few days and the scene in our village is of a winter wonderland as we set out for the hospital. It feels like Christmas Day with the snow outside and the child-like sense of anticipation.

Today's the day we are driving in to have our baby delivered. For the first time in seven years, hospital will be somewhere we go temporarily and to have our souls enhanced, rather than chipped away.

The car's engine has been running for a while, the heaters on full, as I help Georgie out to the car.

TWO FOR JOY

We settle into the car and set out up the country lane from our house. Snow blankets the road and fields around us, the sky a heavy slate colour. I reach across and hold Georgie's hand as we creep slowly along the lane, our tyres crunching through the fresh snow, that and the engine the only noise in this otherwise silent scene.

My mind is a jumble of feelings. I feel so happy, so excited and so apprehensive about what the future might hold.

After a cautious drive through the wintry countryside we arrive in Oxford and pull up at the John Radcliffe. My heart is thumping, racing in anticipation of this big event.

We are shown to the ward, where Georgie undresses and sits up on the bed. I sit next to her and take her hand. She is shaking.

'OK?' I say.

'Yup,' she smiles back, but she looks terrified.

A nurse arrives from the anaesthetic team to talk to us about the procedure. As she starts to talk, Georgie begins to cry.

The nurse sits down on the bed beside us and takes Georgie free hand.

'Don't worry,' she soothes. 'I've read your notes. I'm sure that this is a very big deal for you.'

Georgie nods, still trembling.

'Everything is going to be absolutely fine,' she says. 'We're the best in the business. Just think, in a few minutes from now, you're going to meet your daughter.'

Georgie smiles and I wonder what she must be feeling. Utter terror after what happened last time, but again the steely determination to do the best that she can for her as yet unborn child.

Eventually we are told it's our turn and we make our way to the delivery theatre.

The walls are a garish bright orange and along the far wall are chambers, devices and controls which look like they belong in Frank'nfurter's laboratory in the *Rocky Horror Show*. A small group of doctors and nurses has gathered in anticipation of our arrival and their casual demeanour is somehow unnerving – somehow reassuring.

Once again the epidural is administered. This time I know better than to look over the screen at the wrong moment, and soon our daughter is pulled kicking and screaming into the world. A brief check before she is presented to Georgie and then to me.

I can't believe that I'm holding my daughter. A privilege we had waited months to enjoy with the twins is delivered to us immediately. Our bare baby, barely seconds old, totally unencumbered by medical apparatus, lies in my arms and my heart feels like it's going to burst out of my chest it's thumping so hard. Hammering with excitement, with love and trepidation about what the future might bring for this tiny bundle. Rocket scientist? Ballet dancer? Nurse? Teacher? Who cares – she can be a hobo for all I care as long as she is happy every day of her life.

She grasps my finger suddenly and the deliberate purpose of the movement momentarily knocks the wind out of my sails. I suddenly realise that this child will give me something that I have longed for from the twins, but never received, and I can't wait for the day when she will put her arms around my neck.

This time we're prepared and this time we have our names planned. India Grace will be her name. This time the names have no symbolism, no nod to ancestors or future hopes. Just names because we like them.

I step outside into the cold November air to call Mum. This time, there is no worry about what the future will bring, just unbridled joy at the miracle that has been given to us. It's a shared victory – we have all lived the past seven years together and will live the challenging future together too. So this is a moment for celebration.

I stand shivering in the snowy car park and burble excitedly to her about how bonny, beautiful and perfect our daughter is.

'Thank you for everything, Mum,' I say.

'Don't be silly, darling,' she replies.

'You've always been there for me through everything,' I say. 'Forcing us to take holidays when we most needed them, unconditionally loving our twins, even though it was so frightening for all of us.'

'You're a parent now,' she says, her voice cracking. 'You understand why I did it.'

'I do indeed,' I reply. 'But it doesn't make what you've done any less important.'

*

Later I return to the warm, to the maternity suite, to my beautiful, exhausted wife cuddled up in bed with our new baby.

I cross to the bed, kneel down and rest my head on the pillow beside them. India is asleep, snuffling in that way that only new babies can.

'You know I love you, J,' Georgie says.

'I know,' I say casually and she takes my face in her free hand and looks me straight in the eyes as if to emphasise the point.

'Really, I do,' she says.

'I know, me too,' I say.

'I couldn't do it without you,' she says and I know that I feel the same.

'Me too,' I reply. 'I couldn't function. It's all about you, George. It always has been.'

And I realise that this has been a story as much about love as anything. It's Georgie's courage and determination that has given life to this child. And it's the same courage and determination that has allowed our twins the chance to evolve and develop into the wonderful characters that they are today.

She's the one who kept the twins on board for those critical few days before they were born, nearly killing herself in the process, she's the one who has fought endless battles to get the best for them and she's the one who has been with them every moment, entertaining them and giving them joy and hope through every single exhausting day.

India is her richly deserved reward, her triumph, her victory and I'm lucky to have a share in it.

A magpie flutters up and perches on the frozen window sill: *One for sorrow.*

I smile and watch the bird as its black head twitches from side to side, surveying the bare branches of the trees beneath the window and the Oxfordshire hills blanketed in snow beyond. The lone magpie holds no fear, no sorrow for me now.

Our twins have brought us so much: us parents, our families, friends and everyone whose lives they have touched.

But above all they have brought us all such unexpected joy.

Acknowledgements

First and foremost, thank you to our families; to our parents, sisters, brother and their other halves and children, for the support and love you have shown us and our children. Thank you also to our friends, especially those we have entrusted to be godparents to these special children and to the way that you have responded to that challenge.

There are so many amazing people who have been involved in the care of the twins, from the beginning, when care simply meant survival and getting through the next hour, to their later lives when the twins have required nurture and patience to achieve so many breakthroughs. I'm not even going to attempt to name everyone – that would require another book in itself – so let's stick to the institutions and departments that have played such a key role in this story.

Also a huge thank you to colleagues at FTI Consulting who

ACKNOWLEDGEMENTS

have taken the strain when I have, by necessity, been absent from work, and to the clients, media and other contacts who have been so understanding and supportive.

Thank you to everyone at Wooden Spoon House; to all the social services, physiotherapy, speech and language, occupational therapy and special education specialists at Lambeth Borough Council; to Stuart Korth, everyone at Maytree Primary, Small Steps, WhizzKidz, Helen House, Treloar School, Mary Hare School, Brainwave, Scotson and the Diamond Riding Centre.

Our heartfelt thanks to the amazing people working in the NHS – at Guy's and St Thomas' to everyone on the neonatal unit, the complex motor disorders team (especially the indefatigable Dr Lin), Savannah neuro ward, the paediatric intensive care unit, the high dependency unit, the renal team, the audiology team, the cochlear implant surgery team; the neurological surgery team at King's College Hospital; to the obstetrics team and the paediatric ward at the John Radcliffe; to the A & E staff and paediatric ward at Colchester Hospital; to the paediatric, ophthalmology, orthopaedics and audiology and A & E staff at Stoke Mandeville Hospital; and also to the AMT team at St Thomas' Hospital who have poured so many restorative coffees for us over the years.

Thank you to all of the amazing people at PACE for taking on the twins and for enabling them to achieve so much, despite the odds. We will never forget the formative contribution that you made.

Thanks to all of the carers who have come to support us at home, particularly Karina, Barbara, Iveta, Helen, Emma, Jasmine and most of all Kelly. Thank you for your loyalty, thank you for sticking with us through thick and thin and thank you for being part of our family, even if we do have a few screws loose.

Thank you to Toby Buchan and Chris Mitchell at John Blake Publishing, to Eve White and Helen Bryant for your guidance and for setting me along the right path with the book.

Finally, thank you to Georgie, Thomas, Alice and India for lighting up my life and for giving me new and wonderful experiences every day.